A Personal Journey with the Music of Bob Dylan
by Chris Morris

Chris Morris's approach is founded on informed passion. As a longtime respected music writer...he knows way more about music than most humans, and throughout the book shares enough facts to frame the story neatly into the context of Dylan's career. But he also brings real passion. Instead of an objective book about Dylan and his history (which has already been done countless times), we get this journey through all of Dylan's albums, from the first onward. Each is wrapped around Morris' feelings concerning each album and their station in his life, colored by the often dark, raw realities of his personal passage. — Paul Zollo, author of *Songwriters on Songwriting*, in *American Songwriter*

* * *

I can't think of a better guide through the brilliant, complicated and sometimes baffling career of Bob Dylan than Chris Morris. His wise, wild, personal, and often funny takes on Mr. Dylan's gargantuan recorded history are guaranteed to enlighten, inspire and start an argument or two. — Dave Alvin

* * *

Too many Bob Dylan books have been written with no emotional connection to the songs; too few have been written by those who heard each album as they were released. At its best, Chris Morris' writing achieves what only Dylanologist Paul Williams did before him: It focuses on the songs rather than the man and brings a personal connection that draws the reader closer. The intertwining of Dylan's best records with the highs and lows of Morris' personal life made me chuckle and cry with empathy. An essential slice of Dylan-based lit. — Pat Thomas, author of Listen, *Whitey! The Sounds of Black Power 1965-1975* & *Did It! Jerry Rubin: An American Revolutionary.*

* * *

One of the best music writers of my lifetime. — Mikal Gilmore, *Rolling Stone* contributing writer and author of *Shot in the Heart*

TOGETHER
THROUGH
LIFE

*A Personal Journey with
the Music of Bob Dylan*

TOGETHER
THROUGH
LIFE

*A Personal Journey with
the Music of Bob Dylan*

by Chris Morris

ROTHCO PRESS • LOS ANGELES, CALIFORNIA

Published by
Rothco Press
8033 West Sunset Blvd., Suite 1022
Los Angeles, CA 90046

Copyright © 2017 by Chris Morris
Second edition.

Cover design by Rob Cohen
Cover photo by Michael Ochs Archives
Back cover photos:
Mike June's tattoo, photo © 2016 by Joel Aparicio.
Author photo by Markus Cuff

Rothco Press is a division of Over Easy Media Inc.

ISBN: 978-1-941519-99-8
Electronic ISBN: 978-1-945436-18-5

FOR
Connie
Deirdre
Amy
Ruby
Michele

Redheads all

Time is your soul mate.

— Bob Dylan, 2015

FOREWORD

The most important part of art is not what it gives you, but how you receive and use that art. In my case, no matter what dark or light mood passes through me, the music I listen to seems to change automatically according to my various mood swings. I can never understand how a simple song can reflect one's thoughts for the day. The beauty of pop is that it is both a reflecting pool as well as a statement. A pop song or album can exist on its own, but when a listener approaches that song or album, it becomes a personal conversation between the listener and the artist.

Nöel Coward's great quote "Extraordinary how potent cheap music is" rings often painfully true in my case, and I suspect it does in Chris Morris' case as well. The beauty of reflection is often portrayed in either poetry or music. Both mediums speak to the individual in an intimate manner. Chris, in this wonderful book, is going through a journey of sorts, and on that journey to who knows where, so is Bob Dylan.

Although I greatly admire Dylan, I'm not a big fan of his music. What I do love about him is his sense of theater and his stance as a performer. I think he sees himself as an actor and takes various roles in his life: "folksinger," "rock 'n' roll star," "songwriter," "author," and, most recently, the older sideshow cowboy artist who travels throughout the world in a never-ending manner. Fifty or so years of Bob Dylan, and to this day we really don't know him. That mutating canvas can build a relationship between the fan and artist. It's not a love affair or even a deep friendship, but instead is a guiding beacon to look at in the stars, as if you're seeking a sign that can lead you out from the darkness to the light. Dylan is often put in that navigating position, which is ridiculous, but also profound. What is an artist, except an exceptional human who has the voice one can marvel on, or in this case, a history one can share?

Dylan is not Dylan alone. He's a symbol of many things, the ultimate 20th-century figure who looked back for inspiration, but always stayed in the present tense. Yet, as he traveled and wrote, he added characters and positions that are ever-changing. The beauty of this book is that it is not about Dylan, but about how Chris receives Dylan's work album-by-album, and how his life has reflected that art, as a signpost from one destination to another. Girlfriends and wives may go, times may change, but Dylan is a constant in Chris' life and work.

One of my favorite films is *Orpheus* by Jean Cocteau. There is a scene in the film in which Jean Marais, playing a very well established poet, is listening to his car radio to hear messages or poems from another world. It is mysterious, haunting, and wonderful at the same time. Music is basically signals that we subjectively obtain and digest in a manner where it becomes profound, comforting, or an entrance to a new or different world. Chris is not only a long-term fan of Dylan's music, but he also critically makes judgments on its worth. There are many bumps on this highway, and that is what makes for an interesting life, depressing at times, but with hope and with some joyfulness as well.

As a child of the 1960s I purchased every release from *Bringing it All Back Home* to *New Morning*, for one could not possibly ignore Dylan's presence. I loved him as an icon — not as a leader, but more of a person of taste who brought interesting food to the table. I didn't taste the food through his music, but more by reading interviews with him, and through one striking photographic portrait after another. The beauty of this book is how Chris tastes each meal, each Dylan album, and how it affects or reflects his world at the time of its release.

Marcel Proust tasted the *petite madeleine* and a flood of involuntary memories produced his masterpiece *À la recherche du temps perdu*. The popular song usually places the listener to a precise location and emotional state. Dylan is the voice being broadcast in the car radio, or the chauffeur of Chris's emotional memories — and with that, we're in the car with Chris.

There is a natural tension between what the artist produces, and what the critic comments on. Critical writing is one voice in this book, with the side dish being a memoir. The beauty of all of this is when memory become part of the process, and that is what is both interesting and enjoyable about this book. I'm getting either an introduction to Dylan's art or an opportunity to revisit it, as well as the memories being expressed in Chris' writing. I love both worlds. Now you have it all in front of you.

Tosh Berman
March 5, 2015

4 Chris Morris

INTRODUCTION

Bob Dylan will never be solved, and I am not here to solve him.

In more than 35 years as a working journalist writing about music, I have never been vouchsafed an interview audience with Dylan. This has never been a great disappointment to me; I always figured I'd be too nervous to do the job well, and I assumed that he would simply lie to me anyway. Among his breed, he is the great sleight-of-hand artist, a sly and slippery Melvillean confidence man and shape-shifter, a man possessing an obsession with privacy so extreme that he hid the existence of two wives and at least one daughter from the public.

Some of my friends have played with Dylan. A few of them – bassists Gregg Sutton and Tony Marsico and the late keyboardist Ian McLagan – have even written books that talk about the experience. As good as those books are, none of them casts more than a sliver of light on this most gnomic of artists. Even with his creative intimates, Dylan keeps a wary and self-protecting distance. The Texas guitarist Denny Freeman, whom I've known for 20 years, worked with Dylan for the better part of a decade. He told me that probably the longest conversation he ever had with his boss took place on the day he got fired.

So I do not look to testimony (whether first- or second-hand) or history (and there are library shelves full of it) for the truth of Bob Dylan. Even his own book, 2004's *Chronicles Volume One*, is filled with half-truths, distortions, and outright fictions – disarming and entertaining ones, to be sure, but far from anything we might consider gospel. It has always struck me that it is within what matters most about Dylan, his music, that the great and ultimate truth resides. Much of it is resistant to pure analysis, and hence that truth becomes a personal one. Over the course of more than half a century, I have developed my own sense of that truth, which you will find in these pages.

***

This book was written because I could not finish another one. In the late spring of 2012, the University of Texas Press hired me to write a book about the Los Angeles band Los Lobos for their American Music series. I had a year to deliver the manuscript, but by fall of 2013 I was completed mired in the process and nowhere near completing the work. Weeks would go by, and I would stare with horror at the stack of untranscribed cassettes on my worktable and quickly try to find something else to do. I was, in a word, blocked.

Serendipitously, on Nov. 5, 2013, Sony Music's Legacy division released *The Complete Album Collection Vol. 1*, a CD boxed set comprising Dylan's 41 "official" studio and live albums released between 1962 and 2012, plus a two-CD set of rarities, which is not considered here. (The archival "Bootleg Series" sets were not included, and will likely make up a second boxed collection sometime in the future.) I owned most of the records already, but some I hadn't had for years, and at least one, the shameful 1973 compilation *Dylan*, had never been issued in the U.S. on compact disc. So, without so much as a moment's hesitation, I laid my money down on the counter at Amoeba Music in Hollywood and headed home to dig in.

I began to dutifully work my way through the set, listening to the albums in the order they were released. I had heard all of them pretty much as they came out beginning with 1963's *The Freewheelin' Bob Dylan*, so in a way I was again experiencing them as I had over the course of the previous 50 years. As I listened, an itch swiftly developed, and I realized that the only way to scratch it was to write something about each record after carefully auditioning it again, sometimes several times. I also realized that writing *anything* might be a way to kickstart renewed effort on the Los Lobos project.

I published the work on my Tumblr page "chris morris' wasted space," which had previously been the receptacle for personal writing that was inappropriate for my regular print outlets, or reprints of older and in some cases out-of-print writing that had fresh pertinence. The pieces were labeled "A Dylan a Day," since I posted one every Monday through Friday, from Nov. 6, 2013, to Jan. 3, 2014. I addressed all the albums in the box in order of release except for *Christmas in the Heart*, which naturally had to roll out on Christmas morn.

The form of these stories quickly took shape. They were not so much reviews, really; I had reviewed many of them as they landed, in most cases using a fairly standard critical voice. The *Freewheelin'* piece I posted on Tumblr was a kind of model for everything that followed: It was a highly personal take on the music, a memoir through music, almost. The pieces were not about Dylan and they were not about me; they were about Dylan and me. I found myself reconsidering my past through these records. *Where was I when this came out? How old was I? Where was I living? Who was I with? Was I in love? Was I happy? Miserable? Crazy? Was I high? Where was I working? What was my state of mind? How did the music affect me?* In some cases the pieces were coolly measured (though never impersonal); in others I found myself plunging into places within me that I hadn't visited for years. I was retrieving a portion of my life, which I had spent almost all of in the company of Bob Dylan's music. It was a gratifying experience, and it revealed much to me in the process.

That process became interactive as I posted links to the Tumblr pieces on my Facebook page. I had feared that some might think this a strictly solipsistic and maybe even egomaniacal endeavor, but several of my Facebook friends – some of whom I'd known personally for years, some of whom I knew only as small pictures on my page – responded with comments of their own. Some of them would post something almost every day. Sometimes I'd sit in front of my computer and marvel at the remarkable recollections and observations – even the ones I disagreed with — that my readers would post there. With my Dylan mission complete, I returned to the Los Lobos book, and finally delivered a manuscript in the spring of 2014; it was published as *Los Lobos: Dream in Blue* last fall.

***

Just as I began to prepare this book for publication, I finally caught up with David Kinney's wonderful 2014 book *The Dylanologists: Adventures in the Land of Bob*. I think it occupies a special place on the groaning Dylan bookshelf, and I urge you to pick it up. It is an especially resonant work, and it goes about its business in a fashion unlike any of the others about its oft-surveyed subject.

Kinney, who is a working journalist with the 2005 Pulitzer Prize for breaking news coverage to his credit, moves down the well-trodden path of Dylan's personal and creative history by viewing the musician through the eyes of his fans. They number among them collectors, archivists, obsessives, and pests; many of them are "Bobheads," the peripatetic tribe that attends Dylan's concerts with the same voracity that the Deadheads of old tracked their beloved Grateful Dead. They are scholarly, smitten, acquisitive, combative, resourceful, quixotic, at times delusional. In Kinney's pages one even finds a murder victim among their number.

In the wake of my own labors in the Dylan canon, I read Kinney's book with not a small quotient of self-recognition; my copy became dog-eared as I found one passage after another in which I encountered myself. In its last pages, I found Elizabeth Wolfson, a longtime listener who had some synchronistic experiences not unlike my own:

"Look, I've been listening to [Dylan] since I was fifteen years old. That's a lifetime. The passion has never wavered." Blood On the Tracks, *the record he wrote while his marriage disintegrated, was the soundtrack to her first breakup.* Time Out of Mind, *the 1997 album soaked in regret,*

appeared as her own marriage fell apart. ("It was so potent I could barely listen to it.") "Forgetful Heart" appeared as another relationship was ending. In between, there were all the songs about unrequited love.

This extreme identification with Dylan's words and music, an infatuation that at times has led some listeners into a kind of mad love, is manifested in various ways, often even more extreme, in Kinney's book. He interviews the man who owns the high chair Bob Dylan sat in when he was a baby. Several of his subjects own voluminous archives of bootlegs and concert performances, some of which have literally crowded their owners out of their own homes. The most questing souls follow Dylan's Never-Ending Tour from continent to continent, trailing the master like the acolytes of some seer. Which I suppose Dylan is in the end. And some burrow endlessly and relentlessly, and no doubt fruitlessly, into the guts of Dylan's work, hoping for that elusive "skeleton key in the rain" that will unlock the mysteries of his oeuvre in its totality.

I think it's safe to say that many of those who commented on my pieces about Dylan's albums when they first appeared online are similarly absorbed. My readers proved to be just as opinionated as I am, and some surprised me with their views: I still have a hard time reconciling the affection and admiration that a good friend of 30 years has for the 1988 album *Down in the Groove*, which for me plays like some kind of horrific psy-ops experiment. I know that my Facebook comrades have private archives of their own: Within days of writing about Dylan's 1974 tour with the Band, a CD of the show I attended arrived in my mailbox.

My tastes and my aims, as expressed in these pages, are humble. I am a mid-level Dylanologist at best, Over the years, I've owned just a handful of Dylan bootlegs, and largely have restricted my listening to the original album canon (and its official codicils, the Bootleg Series). This seems to me to be enough, for the released work is a well so deep and impenetrable that I will never be able to fully embrace it or decode it. And, of course, anyone who listens to Bob Dylan's music hears it in a singular way.

My feelings about Dylan's work, and what should be known and not known of it, are expressed in Kinney's summation of the feelings of Michelle Engert, a young woman (and, fittingly, a fellow Chicagoan) who wound up transcribing the small red notebook containing the handwritten drafts of the lyrics for *Blood On the Tracks* for a wealthy collector: *"Dylan delivered a record; wasn't that enough for fans?"*

***

The "A Dylan a Day" entries appear here as they originally appeared; I have resisted the temptation to change or fine-tune them, for I think they stand at their truest as I wrote them, quickly and from the heart.

The only chapters that have not appeared to date are the ones about *Shadows in the Night* and *Fallen Angels*, which were released until after the last of my original Tumblr and Facebook posts. They are far longer than the rest for several reasons. First, I was not shackled by time constraints – the original posts were written on a self-enforced daily deadline – and I felt that these albums deserved a deeper reading, since they is so unlike anything else in the Dylan canon. Also, as you will learn, their appearances coincided with some intense personal events that dovetailed naturally – all too naturally, in fact – with the songs on the albums. Once again, as he often had before, Bob Dylan showed up exactly when I needed him, and not a millisecond too soon.

***

Some thanks are in order here. Thanks to Rob Cohen and Christine Roth for giving my book a second, welcome home. Eternal gratitude goes out to my ever-understanding editor Casey Kittrell of the University of Texas Press and the American Music series editors, Peter Blackstock and David Menconi, who were patient enough to let me pursue this work while their own book sat on the sidetrack. My dear long-suffering friend Tom Cording of Sony Legacy and Dylan's longtime press representative Larry Jenkins, who got *Shadows in the Night* and *Fallen Angels* into my hands well before their release. My sons Max and Zane were my sword and shield.

After some consideration and discussion, I decided that there was no way to seamlessly utilize any of the many, many wonderful comments that were posted on my Facebook page when "A Dylan a Day" first ran. You can still find them there if you're willing to do some scrolling. I'd like to acknowledge the input of some of my constant readers there: Pat Thomas, Bryan Thomas, Bill See, Willie Aron, Rick Campbell, Bill Holdship, Rob O'Connor, Paul Duane, Chuck Prophet, Steve Hochman, Jay Statman, John Swenson, David Jenkins, Dave Soyars, Nick Hill, Tim Stegall, Jack Sherman, Tom Lunt, Bob Collum, Carl DiOrio, Marty Jourard, Al Stewart, Dale Daniel, Mikal Gilmore, Jeffrey Robert Wolfe, Tom Wilt, Jim Testa, Chris Willman, Boris Menart, Benjamin Krepack, Bob Ricketts, Paul Metsa, Jeff Bozem, Saul Davis, Nick Loss-Eaton, Jim Sullivan, Kenny Shiffrin, Bob Mehr, Shawm Brydon, Renaldo Migaldi, Toby Byron, Billy Cioffi, Don McLeese, Steve Barton, Michael Gershberg, Doc Wendell, Jackson Griffith, Norman Maslov, Billy James, Thom Duffy, Denise Cox, Ric Ovalle, Ronee Blakely, Tim Sommer, Bill Knoedelseder, Eric Ambel, Walter Daniels, Marc Platt, Tom Cheyney, Gregg Geller, Paul Body, Mindy Giles, Greg Preston, Jonathan Taylor, Greg Wall, Rick Lawler, and Bob Bell. Special thanks go to David Gorman, who republished the entry about *Oh Mercy* on the great Trunkworthy site. If your name doesn't appear here, it doesn't mean I don't love you.

And special thanks to my beloved friend Nadia Protsenko, who said "I love you" at just the right time.

Bob Dylan

L ook at that cherub on the cover. Barely 20, with baby fat rounding his cheeks. Hard to identify the face with the wizened, rasping 75-year-old of today. His high-collared fleece-lined jacket makes him look slightly vulnerable, as if bundled up for the New York cold, and the cap lends an elfin touch. (Chaplin's Little Tramp was an obvious avatar.) But there's a cool challenge in his gaze, one on which he would swiftly make good.

Recorded live by John Hammond (Senior) in two 1961 sessions for a little more than $400, *Bob Dylan* is at once a pure product of the New York folk revival scene and something that extends beyond that environment. There are 13 songs here, and of them 11 are either traditional or drawn from the folk and blues recordings favored by the folkies of the day. But there's nothing polite or respectful about the performances. No Kingston Triage here. At times, Dylan can't suppress the chuckle that rises out of his throat; at others he howls at the moon and thrashes his acoustic guitar (are you there, Robert Johnson?). He already seems ancient, an elder in a manchild's body. The most transfixing performances are about death – "In My Time of Dying," "See That My Grave Is Kept Clean." Some numbers had been appropriated from other singers' repertoires, but no matter – he stamped them with his own hot brand. Play Dylan's "House of the Rising Sun" next to Dave Van Ronk's, and the younger singer trumps the older folk artist with the insouciant flick of a wrist. Though still a relative novice, Dylan sings like a committed artist.

There are only two originals, and both owe their existence to his exemplar Woody Guthrie. "Talkin' New York" is a talking blues in the Guthrie manner, about Dylan's scuffling days in the clubs and basket houses of what he mockingly calls "Green-witch Village." He would revisit this material, dissembling all the way, in prose 43 years later in his *Chronicles Volume 1*. "Song to Woody" is a tip of the peaked cap to the musician who taught him so much about performing, writing, and self-mythologizing. Within a year and a half, his vaulting ambition would drive his music beyond Guthrie's, in terms of reach and cultural immediacy.

This was the only Dylan album I didn't hear at roughly the same time it came out. I'm not sure what I would have made of it. Reared in a good Commie household, I was already familiar with Leadbelly, "This Land is Your Land," and Pete Seeger's banjo. As a boy I was led by the hand to folk concerts at the University of Chicago and listened to "The Midnight Special" on WFMT. But no doubt the record would have jarred me had I heard it upon its release. Even saintly Pete was by comparison commercial – after all, Gordon Jenkins, later Frank Sinatra's producer, had crafted the Weavers' pop hits. Dylan arrived with an otherness attached to him, despite his status as a major-label recording artist. He already possessed the *yawp*.

Even in its day, Bob Dylan was a rara avis. Somewhere across town, Albert Grossman was putting together Peter, Paul & Mary. Therein lies another tale.

Released March 19, 1962

"You're No Good"
"Talkin' New York"
"In My Time of Dyin'"
"Man of Constant Sorrow"
"Fixin' to Die"
"Pretty Peggy-O"
"Highway 51"
"Gospel Plow"
"Baby Let Me Follow You Down"
"House of the Risin' Sun"
"Song For Woody"
"See That My Grave is Kept Clean"

The Freewheelin' Bob Dylan

I can tell you the exact date I first heard *The Freewheelin' Bob Dylan*: November 22, 1963.

Some kids were crying in homeroom as we watched Cronkite report on what had happened in Dallas, and they let us leave school early. It was the quietest bus ride I ever took. When I got home, I was still upset. My mother knew what to do. She handed me a package she had already wrapped, saying, "I was going to give you this for Christmas, but open it now." I could tell from its shape and heft that it was an LP – the first I'd ever owned myself. And there it was: Dylan walking through the Village slush with Suze Rotolo, shoulders hunched against the gale. Years later, in college, I wore a jacket exactly like the one he's wearing there.

I took the album over to the mono record player, which was housed in an immense TV-phonograph-radio console of dark wood, furniture really, and put it on. And out of the speaker came that frank, unadorned, unsweetened voice, singing a song I knew from Peter, Paul & Mary's version, a radio hit in Chicago that summer. (Mom, an old Red and union maid who still had her songbooks of labor songs, would sometimes go to the Gate of Horn, the folk club run by Dylan's manager Albert Grossman, to hear Miriam Makeba and the like. She loved PP&M, and she owned everything they had released.) My ear was struck anew by the dream-spinning lyrics: "How many seas must a white dove sail before she sleeps in the sand." The beginning of a love affair.

Listening again now, I'm struck by the completeness of Bob Dylan on *Freewheelin'*, even though it was just his second release. He could be tender, thoughtful, rueful, poetic; he could also be loud, raucous, ridiculous, and even vicious. He was only 22 when the album was released, yet he already seemed fully formed,

self-assured, in total command of language and certain about
the right way to present his material. An artist in every cell of
his being. Except for "Corrina, Corrina" – a blues adaptation
which (save for the obscure, rocking 1962 single "Mixed Up
Confusion") presented Dylan in a band setting for the first time
– the album comprised original songs, some derived from Childe
ballads, some drawn from the blazing forge of Dylan's imagination, and all performed solo.

Even if I couldn't then comprehend what the songs were
about – in my early teens, my idea of politics was positively primitive, and I was far too young to have truly loved, or to have loved
and lost – I could tell he knew what he was singing about. And
I understood the world was troubled: I remembered my history
teacher Mrs. Bohnen crying openly in class during the Cuban
missile crisis, when air raid drills had become a regular event. I
had ducked and covered with the rest. I knew this was the world
Dylan was singing about.

But there were no headlines in Dylan's songs, apart from
"Oxford Town," inspired by James Meredith's travails at Ole
Miss, one of his few purely topical compositions and thus
maybe the least effective track on *Freewheelin'*. The tumult and
uncertainty of the day was addressed (*pace* Phil Ochs) in meta-
phor. Little more need be written about "Blowin' in the Wind,"
a song that suggests more than it actually says, a lyrical flight that
struck a universal nerve. "A Hard Rain's A-Gonna Fall" may have
been inspired by the Cuban standoff, but now it plays like the
Apocalypse as painted by Salvador Dali; lyrically it prefigured the
lavish hallucinations that would issue from Dylan's pen in 1965-
66. The insistent "Masters of War" was a bile-spitting indictment
of the military and its industrialists, but it has retained its fire; for
some reason I think of Dick Cheney every time I hear it now.
"Talking World War III Blues," a post-nuclear last-man-on-earth
narrative written in the Guthrie manner, is like a musical "On
the Beach," with jokes; I still laugh when I hear Dylan say, "I lit

a cigarette on a parking meter and walked on down the road." What an image.

As the Minutemen later noted, Bob Dylan may have written propaganda songs, but that was not his only dimension; he would not still be writing and playing today, and we would not be listening today, if it were. Some of the best songs on *Freewheelin'* are about love, and about its betrayals and reversals. His first of many kiss-off tunes, "Don't Think Twice, It's All Right," was inspired by cover girl Rotolo's exit from his life for a year of school in Italy. It cut him to the quick, and, pretty as it is, there is blood in every note. (There's a fleeting but very specific and damning reference to her abandonment in another, lesser track on the album, "Down the Highway.") Then there is "Girl From the North Country," which still causes a catch in the throat with its recollection of a distant love, inspired by an old Minnesota girlfriend. Some of the more sophisticated but still yearning songs he would write in 1974 for *Blood On the Tracks* evoke the same deep feeling.

The rest of the record is in retrospect somewhat ephemeral and not completely realized, but the whole of it captivated my 13-year-old mind. I knew about Elvis, Little Richard, and Jerry Lee, listened to WLS playing rock 'n' roll on my little white transistor radio, but here was a musician who had something to say and said it in his own words, and all he really needed was a guitar. He was...heroic. Like many boys my age, I needed a hero, especially on that day, and I had gotten one, on a 12-inch slab of vinyl.

Released May 27, 1963

"Blowin' in the Wind"
"Girl From the North Country"
"Masters of War"
"Down the Highway"
"Bob Dylan's Blues"

"A Hard Rain's A-Gonna Fall"
"Don't Think Twice, It's All Right"
"Bob Dylan's Dream"
"Oxford Town"
"Talking World War III Blues"
"Corrina, Corrina"
"Honey, Just Allow Me One More Chance"
"I Shall Be Free"

The Times They Are A-Changin'

S
ometime in early 1964, I bought a copy of this glum album with probably around three bucks of my own money, I believe at the local Sears, which is where many people got their LPs in that day. I still feel a little shortchanged.

This has never been a Dylan record I've listened to frequently, or with a great deal of pleasure. I'm sure my mom, who found its left-tilting sentiments appealing, liked it more than I did. It was probably the collection that for all time nailed poor Bob with the "Voice of His Generation" mantle, which he assumed with as much comfort as he might have a hairshirt. A thing much of its time, it's cold and utterly humorless. The high spirits that animated so much of *The Freewheelin' Bob Dylan* are utterly absent.

Some of the songs (and all of them were originals, for the first time) are little more than museum pieces today. "Only a Pawn in Their Game," which uses the 1963 murder of the NAACP's Medgar Evers as a springboard for observations about the mechanics of hate, is protest music trapped in amber. "With God On Our Side" is a bluntly didactic history lesson. "North Country Blues," while prescient in its view of labor outsourcing, is not engaging listening; I didn't even remember it existed until I listened to it today. Even the still-revered "The Lonesome Death of Hattie Carroll," Dylan's recounting of the Baltimore slaying of a black maid by the privileged scion of a wealthy family, is poisoned by its self-righteous tone. This is the stuff that Dylan would himself shortly condemn as "one-dimensional songs" or "finger pointing songs." And he was right about them.

There are good songs here, however, though there is scant warmth in them. "Boots of Spanish Leather," another pretty, sullen number prompted by what Dylan perceived as his girlfriend Suze Rotolo's faithlessness, is nonetheless an affecting personal reflection with a great twist in its tail. The regretful "One Too Many Mornings," which may have similar roots, has abided as an early classic, rightfully, for its hushed beauty. The rabble-rousing title song and the exuberant "When the Ship Comes In," the latter of which Dylan had performed with his new paramour Joan Baez at the march on Washington the previous August, both endure as potent anthems. And "The Ballad of Hollis Brown," the appalling tale of a horrific mass murder-suicide prompted by a farmer's poverty-induced madness, is a chilly wonder that bears comparison with the antique folk balladry that inspired it. The obsessive guitar figure that propels it inexorably to its conclusion still lashes me into the song.

In the end, *The Times They Are A-Changin'* is so relentlessly dour that it seldom calls a listener's name; my copy sat collecting dust for years. Good intentions and righteous politicking never got anybody dancing.

It's an album in which one can sense self-imposed restrictions, and before the album was released Dylan himself, now lionized by the left yet alienated from it, made it clear that he felt constrained even. At his sodden appearance to accept the Tom Paine Award at the Emergency Civil Liberties Committee awards banquet in December 1963, a month before the record reached stores, he drunkenly told his audience, "There's no black and white, left and right to me anymore."

He had been imprisoned in a skin he would have to shed – the first of many he would slough off – and he did so swiftly. In retrospect, the messy "Restless Farewell," which concludes *The Times They Are A-Changin'*, was an appropriate parting shot, despite Dylan's promise to "remain as I am."

Released January 13, 1964

"The Times They Are A-Changin'"
"Ballad of Hollis Brown"
"With God On Our Side"
"One Too Many Mornings"
"North Country Blues"
"Only a Pawn in Their Game"
"Boots of Spanish Leather"
"When the Ship Comes In"
"The Lonesome Death of Hattie Carroll"
"Restless Farewell"

Another Side of Bob Dylan

Different times: In the early '60s, most recording artists were still contractually obliged to deliver a couple of long-playing albums a year to their labels. Thus we have a sonic graph of Bob Dylan's remarkable development as an artist during that time. Between August 1964 and July 1966 he released four albums, one of them pop's first two-LP set. He was moving at the speed of sound, a one-man vanguard; in comparison, even the Beatles looked like layabouts. *Another Side of Bob Dylan* was the opening shot in a volley that still has no real equivalent in the story of modern popular music.

Personally, I found it bewildering. I bought *Another Side* when it came out in mid-1964, and it collected a lot of dust. I was a kid, and I didn't know what I was listening to. The long songs were difficult to penetrate, the writing befuddling. Only in retrospect would I appreciate its accomplishments.

Today, it's a relief to hear Dylan laugh in the middle of the album's first song, "All I Really Want to Do." After the unrelenting gravity of *The Times They Are A-Changin'*, the levity was welcome. The atmospheric change in his music extended far beyond mere humor; Dylan's self-penned liner notes, which had offered "11 Outlined Epitaphs" on *Times*, now promised "some other kinds of songs."

Though that promise was fulfilled, it wasn't as radical as all that: The LP's first side gave us that deliciously warm opening invitation, a piano blues (Bob must have been listening to his Skip James and Roosevelt Sykes albums), a couple of love songs, one of them animated with the heat of sex. None of them seemed foreign or unduly challenging.

But then, tucked near the end of the side, there was "Chimes of Freedom." Imagine the bafflement of a 14-year-old confronted with its mysteries! But, listening to the song now, its narrative appears obvious to me, despite the luminous extravagances of its language. Chased to cover by a downpour, Dylan hears the tolling of a church bell, experiences an epiphany, and finds himself within the glowing embrace of universal empathy. It's a hair-raisingly intense and beautiful song, one of manifest spirituality. Only later would I learn of its roots in the hallucinatory impressionism of Rimbaud. Nothing, not even the imagistic bombardment of "A Hard Rain's Gonna Fall," had truly prepared Dylan's listeners for it, and there was nothing to compare it to in contemporary songwriting.

It was a personal reinvention, and he addressed that reinvention in the album's other great song, the bold gauntlet toss "My Back Pages." Echoing his statement at the Emergency Civil Liberties Committee dinner in 1963, he wrote, "Lies that life is black and white spoke from my skull." Also: "...I'd become my enemy in the instant that I preach." The "Ah" of the song's refrain is one of realization; the text is about nothing more or less than rebirth. Overturning his pulpit and hurling off his former politicking mantle, which had weighed on his shoulders like heavy chainmail, hunching him like an ancient, he was reaching backward, innocent once more, while striding forward, newly formed, eyes refreshed.

The rest of the album comprises a farmer's-daughter joke, recast with a nubile female Norman Bates in the starring role, and three rejections of varied hues – one of them the agonizing and bitter eight-minute "Ballad in Plain D," a brutal fare-thee-well to his once-beloved Suze Rotolo. (Dylan would later say he regretted ever writing it; he would never be so bluntly unguarded about his emotions again. It was another kind of song that we wouldn't hear again.)

It took me a good long while to catch up with it all, for the songs to settle in. Other musicians were paying attention, though, and it was through cover versions that I began to apprehend Dylan's new music. Though it is wholly acoustic, *Another*

Side of Bob Dylan is the beginning of folk-rock. Over the next two years, the Byrds would cut three of the album's 11 songs, and the Turtles would score a hit with "It Ain't Me Babe." We'd learn that even Hollywood studio rats like Sonny Bono were listening up.

For his part, Dylan had early on cast himself as Woody Guthrie, but he had always wanted to be Little Richard. He would soon be something far richer and stranger than anything Mr. Penniman could have imagined in his own roiling, rocking mind.

Released August 8, 1964

"All I Really Want to Do"
"Black Crow Blues"
"Spanish Harlem Incident"
"Cimes of Freedom"
"I Shall Be Free No. 10"
"To Ramona"
"Motorpsycho Nightmare"
"My Back Pages"
"I Don't Believe You"
"Ballad in Plain D"
"It Ain't Me Babe"

Bringing It All Back Home

In 1965, my listening ritual was this: I'd sit in my room in my rocking chair with my transistor radio, which I'd won three years earlier at a raffle at the Century Theatre in Chicago, plugged into my ear. I bought few records; the top 40 station WLS was my musical lifeline.

It's hard to adequately recapture the sensation I felt that spring when "Subterranean Homesick Blues" burned its way through my ear and into my brain. It wasn't just that I hadn't heard *anything* like that from Dylan before; no one had heard anything like that by anybody before. An electric chant running a curt two minutes and 20 seconds, over almost before it began, yet crammed, overstuffed with mirth, nonsense, and vitality. Rebellion, offered as advice, as penned by Lewis Carroll. What was it? I had no idea.

The uptight folk snob in me, welded to the literally sophomoric aesthetic arrogance that almost all teenagers carry with them like a bookbag, interfered with my understanding and appreciation of *Bringing It All Back Home*, the album kicked off by "Subterranean Homesick Blues," for a long time. I had company, and not the best.

The old Lefties, Stalinist in their bones, who had supported Dylan's early broadsides were already lobbing grenades at him for the hazy, personal new material on *Another Side of Bob Dylan* when *Bringing It All Back Home* hit the streets. Their temperatures spiked when it landed. The new album was an act of total apostasy, from its drolly cluttered cover photo to the seven songs, performed with a clattering rock band, that were thrust into listeners' faces on its first side.

Ah, I love that cover (credited to Daniel Kramer). Here's Dylan, no longer the thoughtful loner of earlier jackets, "at home" with a lush-looking woman (his manager Albert Grossman's wife Sally) stretched out next to him in a harlot-red dress, cigarette in hand, louche and seductive. Petting a cat, Dylan idly thumbs an antique magazine with Jean Harlow on its back cover; he looks at the camera matter-of-factly, like someone with nothing to prove to anybody. Various artistic talismans are scattered around him – albums by Lotte Lenya, Robert Johnson, his folkie pal Eric Von Schmidt, the Impressions; an LP by Lord Buckley sits atop the mantelpiece. A fallout shelter sign and a *Time* magazine with LBJ on the cover lie amid the artsy rubble. Is that Charles Olson's book about Moby Dick sitting next to Dylan? Given the "plot" of "Bob Dylan's 115th Dream," I'd like to think so. (Dylan's favorite Melville was likely *The Confidence Man.*) On the back cover we encounter other accomplices, some of them soon to be displaced: Allen Ginsberg, Peter Yarrow, Joan Baez.

Then there were the rock 'n' roll songs on the first side of the album. Rock 'n' roll songs! Revelations, curses, antic blues, vaudeville gags, feverish love ballads, stone gibberish, shaking all in a row, bang-bang-bang-bang-bang-bang-bang, a fusillade of vision, loosely played and untempered, whipped together in a two days' whirlwind. The clamorous spontaneity of these recordings would shortly be replaced by a more diligent but no less inviting strain of rock, but it's a hell of an opening shot. (I have always adored Bruce Langhorne's playing here; I have to believe that he and Tom Wilson, who produced the sessions, supplied the map for Sterling Morrison's beautiful, subdued work on the Velvet Underground's third album – cf. "She Belongs to Me" and "Mr. Tambourine Man." Sometime in the '80s, I met Langhorne at a party in L.A. He was charming, and I was utterly awe-struck.)

The key number for me may be "Maggie's Farm," a comic kiss-off that served as a personal rebuke to those who would have had Dylan sing in chains. "Come on, cross this line, I dare ya." There's a wonderful scene in D.A. Pennebaker's *Dont Look Back*, filmed in London the month after *Bringing It All Back Home* was released in the U.S., in which Sally Grossman is captured dancing to the song, which spins on the record player like a pro-peller made of sabers, even as the idolatrous folkniks who cir-cled him that season lie in wait for the King of Protest. (They would seek vengeance a year later.) Joan Baez cluelessly responds to Grossman's hip-shake by serenading Grossman with the Jaynetts' "Sally Go 'Round the Roses." Another farmworker still parked in the fields, watching a distant tornado rip across the landscape, Baez was already gone and didn't know it. In those days, if you couldn't keep up, and few could, Dylan would simply leave you standing in the dust. The road would be littered with those left behind, scorned, abandoned, and sometimes mocked. His blood was running at once hot and cold. For a time I would myself stand flat-footed with my schoolboy hat in my hand as he roared past.

The second, acoustic-based side contained four great monoliths of verse, golden and impenetrable. Within months, we would be dancing to the Byrds' clipped version of "Mr. Tambourine Man." Then no one dared essay "Gates of Eden" and "It's Alright Ma (I'm Only Bleeding)," so grand in design and ambition that they defied interpretation. I lack the poetry to wrestle with their explication; those songs are so vast that even now I can only nibble at their edges.

The album closes with the song that Dylan used to quiet the crowd at the Newport Folk Festival that July after he'd stirred them to near-revolt with an electric set. "Look out, the saints are coming through," he cautioned. Then: "Strike another match, go start anew." Within three months, many would take that challenge and thrust Bob Dylan, a one-man riot in song, up the pop charts.

Released March 22, 1965

"Subterranean Homesick Blues"
"She Belongs to Me"
"Maggie's Farm"
"Love Minus Zero/No Limit"

"Outlaw Blues"
"On the Road Again"
"Bob Dylan's 115th Dream"
"Mr. Tambourine Man"
"Gates of Eden"
"It's Alright, Ma (I'm Only Bleeding)"
"It's All Over Now, Baby Blue"

Highway 61 Revisited

"O nce upon a time," the song began, but it was no fairy tale. No, "Like a Rolling Stone" was a six-minute-plus blast of rancor, a pitiless outburst hurled in icy flames, and it came writhing out of the radio that summer like a burnt offering. Majestic and wrathful, it pushed everything else you could hear aside. "How does it feel?" It felt like something utterly new, at least within the sphere in which I was accustomed to listening.

My beloved transistor had by then died an honorable death; after years of abuse, its much-abused diode guts could no longer be constrained by Scotch tape and had finally spilled themselves on my bedroom floor in an act of electronic seppuku. I now listened to our old Zenith tabletop model in the kitchen, taking in WLS's daily top 40 countdown show, the *Silver Dollar Survey*, as I scratched away at my homework after school. Week after week, I scanned the station's printed rundown of the day's hits with something like awe as my onetime folk hero scaled the chart, ultimately settling shy of the top, denied, of course, by the Beatles.

In the day, nothing so dramatically evolved was agitating the airwaves. Here are a few of the songs that reached No. 1 in 1965: "Downtown," "This Diamond Ring," "Game of Love," "I'm Telling You Now," "Mrs. Brown You've Got a Lovely Daughter," "I'm Henry VIII, I Am." The Beatles gave us "Eight Days a Week," "Ticket to Ride," "Help!," and "Yesterday," the Stones "Satisfaction" and "Get Off My Cloud." Others were sprinting to catch up, straining at the mile markers Dylan had already laid down: It was the year of the Byrds' "Mr. Tambourine Man" and "Turn, Turn, Turn!," Barry McGuire's "Eve of Destruction," and, oh Lordy, Sonny and Cher's "I Got You Babe." Dylan was creating in thinner air, but his transmitting tower was taller and more powerful. If the charts were a horse race, "Like a Rolling Stone" was ahead by several lengths, and the jockey was cruising to the line with a quiet whip hand, not even bothering to look over his shoulder.

My memory is cloudy on this point, but I think I bought *Highway 61 Revisited* sometime in late '65. The single had engulfed my imagination. I had of course read accounts of Dylan's stormy appearance at the Newport Folk Festival that year; he had once been the prince of the city there, but he'd brought his holy Fender along and some were now calling for his head on a pike. In my wee 15-year-old mind, I could somewhat understand the furor, for the album was immense and baffling to my ears.

On its cover, Dylan stared frankly into Daniel Kramer's lens, sporting a shirt of opulent proto-psychedelic patterning over a t-shirt advertising Triumph motorcycles. (I was sure his bike was very fast.) He is holding what appears to be a socket wrench in his hand. "Here, kid, you're gonna need this tool to get the job done."

I needed a bigger toolbox. Save its last track, the LP comprised full-bore, full-band rock 'n' roll songs of surpassing elegance and density, upping the ante shoved onto the table with *Bringing It All Back Home*. It was as if Dylan were trying to expunge the word "folk" from his vocabulary, even as writers began to employ that curdled term "folk-rock," first of many uneasy pop hyphenates. The music was prickly and superheated, packed with capering word-bombs, with a sullen undertow of threat, spiked with condemnation. The stiletto slashes of the lead guitarist, whose name was then unfamiliar, was a perfect complement to Dylan's frequent gushes of bile; the player was Michael Bloomfield, and in short order he would become my first guitar hero, thanks to the debut album by the Paul Butterfield Blues Band, the first blues LP I ever purchased. (Much is made of Al Kooper's incursion on organ here, but for me the secret hero of *Highway 61 Revisited* is pianist Paul Griffin, whose ornamental filigrees loft every track he graces.)

By turns hilarious and excoriating, Dylan applied the laugh and the lash in equal measure. He could still be sweet – that baby boy on his first LP cover had not disappeared entirely – and the beauty of "It Takes a Lot to Laugh, It Takes a Train to Cry" and the yearning "Queen Jane Approximately" supply a welcome burnishing touch. Some numbers – "Tombstone Blues," "From a Buick 6," "Highway 61 Revisited" – were antic, swerving blues. But standing out were the venomous "Ballad of a Thin Man," with its doomsday chords, and "Just Like Tom Thumb's Blues," Dylan's *Bateau Ivre*, a drunken *Odyssey* conceived without compass or sextant.

I was probably never tested by a song as I was by the album's closing track, "Desolation Row," the most populous tune on a record that would nonplus a census taker. Stretched to a length of over 10 minutes, it plays like the audio equivalent of Breughel's "The Garden of Earthly Delights." Framed simply by Charlie McCoy's guitar and Russ Savakus' bass, it's an oil spill of allusion that slowly spreads farther from shore with each coiled verse. You could write an entire academic text on the line, "Ezra Pound and T.S. Eliot fighting in the captain's tower/while calypso singers laugh at them and fishermen hold flowers." Cinderella, Romeo, Cain, Abel, the Hunchback of Notre Dame, Ophelia, Einstein (disguised as Robin Hood), the Phantom of the Opera, Casanova, and diverse lesser actors crowd their way into the picture. The library has exploded, and Dylan has picked up the random pages and re-bound them.

Highway 61 Revisited stopped the traffic in my mind as surely as a big red octagonal sign a mile wide. I would file it away, confused, but it traveled with me when I went away to college in 1967, when Dylan presented himself to me most completely, as I flowered in the cutting winds of Wisconsin.

Released August 30, 1965

"Like a Rolling Stone"
"Tombstone Blues"
"It Takes a Lot to Laugh, It Takes a Train to Cry"
"From a Buick 6"
"Ballad of a Thin Man"
"Queen Jane Approximately"
"Highway 61 Revisited"
"Just Like Tom Thumb's Blues"
"Desolation Row"

Blonde On Blonde

I finally got it, but I had to leave home and head up north to school before I did. Drugs were involved, of course. I was finally off my chain. Late at night in Madison, in our rooms in the euphoniously named Ogg Hall, we'd burn a stick of sweet jasmine incense, stuff wet towels into the crack in the bottom of the door, and light one up. The house fellows turned a deaf nose to it all. And so I found myself lofted high enough to sink my ears into what Bob Dylan had recently wrought.

Of course I'd heard the singles that preceded the 1966 release of *Blonde On Blonde*. They had dropped like a string of incendiary devices to blow up the radio, musical napalm: the acid-tongued "Positively Fourth Street," the weedhead anthem "Rainy Day Women #12 & 35," the lustfully persuasive "I Want You," the sublimely beautiful, pitying "Just Like a Woman" (o dear Edie Sedgwick, was that really you?). There was another 45 most people, including myself, had missed: the hectoring, slavering "Can You Please Crawl Out Your Window," which Dylan had cut with his new touring band, a bunch of slamming Canuck rockabillies called the Hawks.

He had wanted to make what became *Blonde On Blonde* with the Hawks, but only managed to record one usable song with them, the levitating "One of Us Must Know (Sooner Or Later)." The group, still all bama-lama pow-pow-pow then, couldn't quite replicate the lustrous sound that Dylan heard in his head, and at his intuitive producer Bob Johnston's suggestion he decamped, with Jaime Robbie Robertson of the Hawks and Al Kooper, to Nashville, where a group of sympathetic Music City session musicians would become well acquainted with the hours between midnight and dawn. It was an album cut from the colors of the darkest morning.

I began to grow nocturnal myself, and after I very belatedly purchased the album at Discount Records down on State Street – where a clerk named Liza stopped my heart every time she worked behind the counter, ah! – *Blonde On Blonde* became a nightly companion. It was probably the first two-LP rock record ever released (though the Mothers of Invention's contemporaneous *Freak Out!* was also a Page House favorite), and it demanded study, long hours of contemplation. What a disciplined young man I was.

My guru of sorts in this regard was a guy named Johnny Klate. He was slightly older, a transfer from New York if I remember right and not interested in academics whatsoever. He was handsome in a chiseled way, and he was cloning Dylan's look (though he couldn't pull off the 'fro with his straight, lank black hair) – leather jacket, straight-leg jeans (no bells on our hooligan), carrying a guitar with him everywhere, affecting a seen-it-all mien and a curled lip. Co-eds launched themselves at him like rocket-propelled grenades. Some nights he'd drop by the room, glassy-eyed, to strum a bit and talk music; he supplied some of the skeleton keys to *Blonde On Blonde*, which we spun on my roommate's Marantz portable stereo, and some of the smoke, too, for he was always holding. Other nights I indulged in stoned, solitary listening.

Wrecked on cheap yet effective pot, I'd stretch on my narrow dorm room bed, vividly conscious of the rising and falling of my breath, and inhale the expanses of that 73-minute cipher, certain that if I listened with that inner ear I was learning to develop, I could unlock its multitudes of secrets. Some of my friends preferred the more brazen sound of *Highway 61 Revisited*, but this one was it for me. I loved its wide-open spaces, its sheer scope, its spectrum of emotion, its enveloping warmth. It was tactile, velvety, my bed of roses.

The record was filled with women. A gallery of Picassos might sound like this if the paintings had voices; the Spaniard, like the Minnesotan, studied women from every angle, and like each plane on his canvases, each note on the record revealed a fresh, sparkling mystery. The first women you encounter, amid what sounds like a party in the studio, are seemingly the kind you hold not in an embrace, but in a roach clip (But we may be mistaken about the meaning of that text. For Dylan, an outcast to many, an outlaw by profession and temperament, no stranger to recent adversity, and familiar with the scriptures, may have been thinking of Deuteronomy 21: "And they shall say unto the elders of his city, This our son is stubborn and rebellious, he will not obey our voice; he is a glutton, and a drunkard. And all the men of his city shall stone him with stones, that he die: so shalt thou put evil away from among you; and all Israel shall hear, and fear.")

The rest in Dylan's gallery parade in and out of the scene with their own narratives, their own glamour and hilarity ("Oh, mama"), some beckoning, some rejected, some dancing madly, some collapsed in a flood of tears. Many receive a ribald, bluesy 21-gun rock 'n' roll salute ("Pledging My Time," "Leopard Skin Pill-box Hat," "Absolutely Sweet Marie"), but the ones I loved and desperately wanted to know are the objects of rough and uncontrollable desire, laid down with a soft caress.

"Visions of Johanna" had defeated Dylan and the Hawks in the New York studio. Some now-familiar outtakes offer up incongruously muscular versions of the song, sometimes tagged as "Freeze Out." But the night played no tricks in those tracks, which would occupy bootleggers for years. He craved that ghost electricity, a sound that ran its fingers through Johanna's hair, and in Nashville he found it with seven-and-a-half minutes of acuity worthy of the song's title. The swell and small bird cries of Al Kooper's organ playing, only now and then poking out of the mix, and the economical snare and hi-hat taps of Kenny Buttrey's drums sweep the track into an ebbing and flowing eddy, but those players and the rest of the band have their true apotheosis in Johanna's companion, "Sad Eyed Lady of the Lowlands."

The song, an 11-minute cyclone of unkempt imagery, had been finally committed to tape not long before the early morning sun started warming the studio door in Nashville. The session musicians had stood around for hours, on the clock, bullshitting and swilling coffee and soda, while Dylan wrestled with his lyrics on the studio floor. It emerged magically, born without precedent, exotic as a bird of paradise, coasting on a swirl of rhythm and the purr of Kooper's Hammond, rising in slow-dawning force as Dylan opened wide his warehouse eyes and Buttrey pounded his Arabian drum.

Might this Lady have been Sara Lownds, whom Dylan had married in late 1965? Does it matter? Let her be whomever you will. There is nothing literal about the song; there is no way to resolve its capacious questions. Knowing it is a love song is enough. Ineffable, seductive, its every phrase and every bar and very form stretching to the limit, it is huge enough to contain any and every woman you or I or anyone else may have loved. Thus it casts the longest shadow of anything its author wrote in this period, or, to my mind, maybe ever.

It would be the last we would hear from Bob Dylan for a time. He'd returned exhausted from a tour of the world, where he was jeered and vilified. His spiritual tank was empty, but his bike was gassed up and he went for a ride. As he looked into the sky searching for a woman's face, riding sunblind at a velocity undreamed of by most even in those cranked-up days, a wall rose up to meet him, and some believed he had come close to death as he fell.

As for myself, in a short time, I would have my own lady of the Milwaukee lowlands. Cindy's eyes were not sad, however, until after she had been with me for a while. One night not long after we met, she took a handful of collegiate speed to study, but instead she wrote me a 20-page love letter. An amphetamine whirlpool brimming with longing, to my smitten eyes it read like it could have been Dylan's unwritten liner notes for *Blonde On*

Blonde, and it filled my heart as surely and as swiftly as I would break hers.

Released mid-July, 1966

"Rainy Day Women #12 & 35"
"Pledging My Time"
"Visions of Johanna"
"One of Us Must Know (Sooner or Later)"
"I Want You"
"Stuck Inside of Mobile with the Memphis Blues Again"
"Leopard-skin Pillbox Hat"
"Just Like a Woman"
"Most Likely You Go Your Way and I'll Go Mine"
"Temporary Like Achilles"
"Absolutely Sweet Marie"
"Fourth Time Around"
"Obviously Five Believers"
"Sad Eyed Lady of the Lowlands"

John Wesley Harding

He had fallen to earth; those wax wings had become two-ended candles burned to a nub. Too close to the sun! He knew we were still looking for him and to him, so he went on the lam and hid out, mainly in basements in the Saugerties, with his gang. There he tried on old songs and new, but we would not hear them until smugglers slipped them to us in snowy-white sleeves. Then without so much as a clarion he reappeared, and had he presented himself naked it would not have been more of a shock.

John Wesley Harding reached stores in late 1967, not long after Christmas. It had been a year and a half since Bob Dylan had released an album. In the interim, many musicians had answered the siren's call of his electric music; it had been the year of "A Whiter Shade of Pale." You could fairly taste the acid in the air, and in the cathedrals of studios, a new extravagance was being concocted every week, often in a manner that had already come to be called "Dylanesque."

But Dylan himself, who hitherto had never viewed the zeitgeist as anything other than a springboard to launch him another 100 miles up the road, materialized out of the ether with a squint and a crooked grin, flanked before bare trees on the cover of his unexpected album by a farmer and two incognito Bengali musicians. The music inside was denuded, impossibly spare, nearly monastic. He had returned to Nashville and re-enlisted Charlie McCoy and Kenny Buttrey, the stalwarts of *Blonde On Blonde*. On 10 of the record's 12 tracks, playing what sounded like only the right notes at the right times, they supplied the sole accompaniment to Dylan's seared acoustic guitar and piano and his austere, cryptic collection of jokes, riddles, and illuminations.

As unadorned as it was, it was at first hard to divine its silenc-
es. Six months later, his erstwhile accomplices, now calling themselves the Band, would release their own unfathomable work,
Music From Big Pink, which contained two songs either written
or co-written by Dylan, wrapped in a cover he painted in the
manner of Marc Chagall. Those two LPs bolstered my world like
bookends over the course of 1968.

I found he had not lost his sense of humor. The howler
was the album's title song and leadoff track, at once a carefully
crafted modern gunfighter saga and a deadpan gloss on badman
balladry. Dylan had no doubt heard his friend and label mate
Johnny Cash's song about John Wesley Hardin on his 1965 concept record *Ballads of the True West*, and he may have read the outlaw's mendacious autobiography, posthumously published after
he received a bullet in the back of his skull in an El Paso saloon,
like someone in a Marty Robbins song. Dylan added a "g" to
Hardin's name, and his saintly alternate-universe gunslinger is a
far cry from the cross-drawing psychopath who may have cut
as many as 40 notches into the butt of his Colt during his ram-
paging, conscienceless career. Anyone who knew the real story
would laugh out loud.

The other songs similarly floated in from another time, set in
a mannered, sometimes deliberately stilted syntax and lingo that
leaned towards the biblical and away from the hallucinatory. The
characters – hobos, drifters, immigrants – would not have been
unfamiliar to anyone who, like Dylan, had read *Bound For Glory*,
but he set his archetypes spinning like tops with their own weird
centrifugal energy. Some, like the lonely figures in "All Along the
Watchtower" and "The Wicked Messenger," appeared to hale
from a time too distant to recall, climbing from a barren, wind-
swept wasteland impossible to locate on a map.

At the first glance the album was all gleaming bone, but
its plentiful sinew revealed itself over months of listening. I
would come to howl at the loose-jointed parable "The Ballad
of Frankie Lee and Judas Priest," in which a frontiersman out

of Samuel Beckett fucks himself to death, expiring in the arms of a man who may or may not be Jesus Christ. Similarly delicious is the cinematic act-of-God comedy that is "The Drifter's Escape," staged on a Western set that would stand on Dylan's artistic backlot for years. "As I Went Out One Morning" seemed to be a play on Dylan's own "Motorpsycho Nightmare," with the script rewritten and the obvious comedy drained from it; its shotgun-toting yokel was now a revolutionary theorist.

There was gravity, too, in the pitiless "I Am a Lonesome Hobo" and "I Pity the Poor Immigrant." In the astonishing "I Dreamed I Saw St. Augustine," Dylan, no longer japing in his sleep as he had on his earliest albums, bemoans his complicity in a martyr's imagined death, and awakens weeping.

Then, just when the dark wood of the album's rigor was beginning to feel oppressive, the pedal steel guitar of Pete Drake, another practiced Nashville hand, admitted an unanticipated beam of sunshine into "Down Along the Cove" and "I'll Be Your Baby Tonight." There is nothing unanswerable in these tunes, one of which audaciously rhymes "moon" and "spoon" in the grand Tin Pan Alley manner, nor does there appear to be irony in them, either. The simplicity of presentation in *John Wesley Harding* had boiled its way down to the lyrics; Dylan was unashamedly writing old-school country love songs, as bold and affecting as anything in the brighter leaves of Hank Williams' book.

Hearing those numbers, you could tell that the Nashville grass felt good between Bob Dylan's toes. He staked a claim where the ground was clear and the air was crisp, far from the hubbub on the psychedelic playground he had helped to build. He would sojourn there for a while.

Released December 27, 1967

"John Wesley Harding"
"As I Went Out One Morning"
"I Dreamed I Saw St. Augustine"

"All Along the Watchtower"
"The Ballad of Frankie Lee and Judas Priest"
"Drifter's Escape"
"Dear Landlord"
"I Am a Lonesome Hobo"
"I Pity the Poor Immigrant"
"The Wicked Messenger"
"Down Along the Cove"
"I'll Be Your Baby Tonight"

Nashville Skyline

The world was in flames, and up stepped Bob Dylan, tipping his hat, holding a glass of lemonade. "Here, have a sip of this, it might cool your brow."

In a season of fury, he had returned to Nashville and re-upped with the crew that had made the elusive, allusive *John Wesley Harding*. But the sound was now bulked up to full-band strength, Dylan's voice was plummy and round where once it had been flat and serrated, and he was singing country songs, or his notion of them. His acolytes had beaten him to the punch: The previous summer, the Byrds had issued *Sweetheart of the Rodeo*, containing plentiful steel guitar, covers of Merle Haggard, George Jones, and Louvin Brothers songs, and versions of two numbers recorded during Dylan's still-fugitive, now-bootlegged home recordings with the Hawks.

It was a bit of a shocker, in spite of a kind of two-song preview on the preceding album. The sound was largely sunny and professional (though still messy around the edges), and Dylan's ripened singing couldn't possibly have been anticipated. After the sprawl of *Blonde On Blonde* and the density of *JWH*, the utter economy of *Nashville Skyline* was flabbergasting: Clocking in at just 27 minutes, you could listen to it twice at lunchtime. And there was even less there than met the eye. Subtract the awkward, flubbed duet with Johnny Cash on the remade "Girl From the North Country" (I loved that song, and was horrified) and the toss-away instrumental "Nashville Skyline Rag," and you could practically consume it during a coffee break. It was the first Bob Dylan album that contained anything inessential.

But for all that, it had its charms, and today there are only a couple of songs – "To Be Alone With You," "Country Pie" – that really seem slight. The best of Dylan's compositions, though lacking the convolutions and chimeras of his earlier stuff, work splendidly; he had instinctively absorbed the country template and manipulated it to his own emotional ends. There wasn't anything fancy or especially crafty in this music, but there was no back-to-the-land corn in it, either, and it contained depths of its own sort.

Lust and regret live here. "Lay Lady Lay" became a top 10 hit, and its naked priapism was completely in tune with the hedonism of the era. The ecstatic "Tonight I'll Be Staying Here With You" moves into similar carnal territory. "I Threw It All Away" is Hank Williams-worthy. In its horror of infidelity, "Tell Me That It Isn't True" suggests that Dylan was familiar with George Jones' "Say It's Not You." Listening now, the biggest surprise is "One More Night." That buoyant, chipper number has a subversive twist of abandonment and betrayal in its tail: "Tonight, no light will shine on me."

People probably took the record as something slightly less than what it actually was, and I believe most did, because Dylan had given them permission to do so. The beaming, bearded rustic on the cover was inviting us in to sit for a spell. Of course the real Dylan would do nothing of the kind, but at that time it felt like it might be pleasant to pull up a chair and listen to some picking. The album came with a welcome mat.

At that precise moment the battle outside was indeed shaking windows and rattling walls; the tumult had escalated since Dylan prophesied the changing of the times only five years earlier. I had already gotten my first whiff of tear gas, and within a year I would be dodging police billy clubs as protests of the Cambodian invasion sparked armed clashes in the streets of my college town, and rioters would be confronted by the National Guard. That summer, four radicals blew up a building on my campus, killing a researcher and snuffing dissent at the school for years.

For me the previous summer of 1969 was a brief idyll between sieges on the battlements. I had moved into a house in

Madison, but was killing time that season in Chicago. I had fallen in, but not fallen in love, with a spoiled Jewish girl from the northern suburbs, the best friend of my best friend's girlfriend, and it became a party in motion. We got stoned and watched a surreal live telecast from the moon, and went to Crosby, Stills, Nash & Young's debut performance at the Auditorium Theatre. She laid me across her parents' bed, which was big but not brass. One weekend, we all drove to Madison. On Saturday afternoon, *Nashville Skyline* played as Linda and I watched mescaline mandalas spin on my living room wall.

Lemonade.

Released April 9, 1969

"Girl From the North Country" (with Johnny Cash)
"Nashville Skyline Rag"
"To Be Alone With You"
"I Threw It All Away"
"Peggy Day"
"Lay Lady Lady"
"One More Night"
"Tell Me That It Isn't True"
"Country Pie"
"Tonight I'll Be Staying Here With You"

Self Portrait

Here we have the first God-knows-I-tried album in the canon. It would not be the last. Surprised listeners had to summon up extraordinary reserves of patience and forgiveness to wade through this two-LP grab bag of unsorted, mediocre music, which arrived with a thud in the summer of 1970. It still requires almost a physical effort to get all the way through it.

Self Portrait is Dylan's junk drawer. I'm willing to bet every kitchen in America has one. Mine contains a hammer, screwdrivers, light bulbs, disused cell phones, a disassembled *Sin City* action figure, assorted loose screws and picture hangers, thumbtacks, blank DVDs, poker chips, a computer mouse, a broken iPod, a miniature baseball bat, extension cords, staples, a flashlight, shipping and masking tape, spare toner, and a set of promotional Def American brass knuckles. There's more, but that's as deep as I could dig.

It was as if Dylan and producer Bob Johnston, both of whom had previously moved with such assurance, went to the tape library, closed their eyes, swept unused tracks off the shelf, tossed them in a box, and shipped them off to the pressing plant.

The artist responsible would himself later maintain that the album was his response to the bootlegging of his unreleased work, which began in July 1969 with the release of *Great White Wonder*, a revealing hodge-podge of a record that every respectable hippie household had to have by the turntable. All Dylan's own mock-bootlegging proved was that he couldn't separate his own wheat from his chaff with any aesthetic acumen. Many would echo *Rolling Stone*'s legendary question: "What is this shit?" Others would say, "Where is the self?"

The whole thing was confused and tentative. At times Dylan hid within his own album, like a desperado cowering behind the rocks amid a shootout: Two of the tracks didn't even feature his own voice, while a third found him idiotically crooning "dah-dah-dah" over tipsy-sounding horns. He tried on others' material in an awkward dress-up: there were two covers of old Everly Brothers songs, and Hank Snow, Elmore James, Gordon Lightfoot, and Guy Mitchell, among others, also loaned their repertoire. There was a certain perverse satisfaction in hearing Dylan overdubbing himself to portray both Simon and Garfunkel on "The Boxer," but it was still terrible. A couple of songs, "Little Sadie" (the source of "Cocaine Blues," unforgettably recorded at Folsom by Johnny Cash just two years earlier) and "Alberta," appeared in a pair of variant drafts, neither of them excellent, in what looked like a desperate make-weight maneuver. Antiquities about gold mining and moonshining were bedecked with incongruous arrangements, folk finery in tatters.

Fans were excited by the prospect of hearing four selections from Dylan's 1969 appearance with the Band, now stars in their own right, at the Isle of Wight Festival. It had been his first full-length gig in three years. But the material – nearly the only stuff written by Dylan himself on the record, and all of it familiar – sounded ghastly, the musicians tentative, the mix confused. Appallingly, Dylan muffs the lyrics to "Like a Rolling Stone." (The awfulness of that show was thrown into bold relief by the bootleg availability of the mislabeled "Royal Albert Hall" show by Dylan and the Hawks, their fearsome, chaotic May 17, 1966 date in Manchester, England.)

None of it cohered; since some selections found Dylan employing his Crosbyesque *Nashville Skyline* voice and others were cut in his old adenoidal style, there appeared to be more than one lead vocalist at the helm. But that's wrong, because plainly no one's hand was really on the wheel, and the entire enterprise headed straight for the rocks.

I listened dutifully, but without focus. I simply didn't have the will. I would listen to Bob Dylan's next album in the day room of a locked ward.

Released June 8, 1970

"All the Tired Horses"
"Alberta #1"
"I Forgot More Than You'll Ever Know"
"Days of 49"
"Early Mornin' Rain"
"In Search of Little Sadie"
"Let It Be Me"
"Little Sadie"
"Woogie Boogie"
"Belle Isle"
"Living the Blues"
"Like a Rolling Stone"
"Copper Kettle (The Pale Moonlight)"
"Gotta Travel On"
"Blue Moon"
"The Boxer"
"The Mighty Quinn (Quinn the Eskimo)"
"Take Me As I Am (Or Let Me Go)"
"Take a Message to Mary"
"It Hurts Me Too"
"Minstrel Boy"
"She Belongs to Me"
"Wigwam"
"Alberta #2"

New Morning

Years after you first hear an album, your response to it is inevitably colored by where you were at spiritually and emotionally when you first listened to it. While *New Morning* is not an especially dark album, I was in a very dark place in late 1970, and thus it's hard for me to apprehend it today with much pleasure, or much clarity for that matter.

You see, I had lost my mind; there is no other way to put it, really. Over the course of the year, my girl had moved out on me and back to Milwaukee, where, I learned later, she entered a convent; my drug and alcohol intake had skyrocketed; and I had been spurned by a beautiful dark-haired woman, a classmate in one of my lit courses, with whom I had impulsively and hopelessly fallen in love. I stopped going to classes, my textbooks were untouched. Exhausted and deranged, one night around Thanksgiving I went to a rehearsal of the theater company I had joined and laid prone on the floor, paralyzed. The next day, after a headache of what I imagine was migraine intensity scorched my brain, one of my roommates drove me to University Hospital, and I checked myself into the psychiatric ward.

One of the roomies thoughtfully delivered my scarcely-played copy of *New Morning* to me during my four-week stay, along with (what could be more perfect?) Robert Johnson's *King of the Delta Blues Singers*. Those albums were soon joined by George Harrison's new *All Things Must Pass*, which I bought while on a rare day pass off the ward a couple of weeks into my stay; it shared with *New Morning* a version of "If Not For You," co-written by Harrison and Dylan, as well as another joint composition, "I'd Have You Any Time."

I would play those albums late at night on the console stereo in the day room, with the volume tuned to a whisper. Johnson's

hellhound was nipping at my own heels, and the glowing expanses of Harrison's record calmed me like a warm bath. It was heavy
rotation for them. But *New Morning* resisted my efforts to enter
it. All I can remember hearing was a couplet – from a love song,
no less:

> *Storm clouds are raging all around my door*
> *I think to myself I might not take it anymore*

The record sounded fine, just fine, certainly better than the
catastrophic and thoroughly condemned *Self Portrait,* which had
preceded it by just a few months. But it was weightless to my ears,
and I couldn't relate to what Dylan was writing about. The love
songs, even one as lustful as the bluesy "One More Weekend,"
made me shudder. The title track was a light year removed from
my reality: My morning found me gazing at a tall pile of slushy
snow outside the hospital window. Jokes like the beatnik spoof
"If Dogs Run Free" left me cold. I didn't give a fuck about
Dylan's honorary degree from Princeton (since at that juncture it
didn't appear I'd be getting a degree from anywhere) or his real
or imagined encounter with Elvis.

But he gave me something, at least, though, circumscribed
by night and feeling deserted by a God I wasn't even certain existed, I was not immediately prepared to hear him. At the close
of his record he presented me with three angels and he offered
me a prayer, and today those songs are capable of lifting me, in
a way nearly all of Bob Dylan's "religious" music never could.

Somehow I began to mend. Declared "well" and discharged,
I went to work in a grocery store, raided the public library, toyed
with therapy, went back to school, and graduated. During my
senior year I met a woman from Florida who had bewitched
me completely, and I moved back to my hometown, where she
tardily joined me.

In those days, in my apartment on Lincoln Avenue, *New
Morning* was seldom drawn down from the shelf. It would then

be a couple years before Bob Dylan completely emerged from a
silence he now imposed.

Released Oct. 21, 1970

"If Not For You"
"Day of the Locust"
"Time Passes Slowly"
"Went to See the Gypsy"
"Winterlude"
"If Dogs Run Free"
"New Morning"
"Sign on the Window"
"One More Weekend"
"The Man in Me"
"Three Angels"
"Father of Night"

Pat Garrett & Billy the Kid

I t wasn't really a "Dylan album," though many wanted one after his three-year absence. The word "soundtrack" appeared prominently in the line at the top of its barren cover; many ignored it. It comprised the music Dylan wrote and performed for Sam Peckinpah's myth-puncturing Western *Pat Garrett and Billy the Kid*.

Bloody Sam at first didn't want Dylan, but upon listening to his music at the insistence of the film's producer, he embraced the musician and cast him in his movie. Only two of the tracks on the soundtrack album, "Knockin' On Heaven's Door" and "Billy 1," were actually songs that appeared in the feature; the rest was incidental music, which the wrathful Jerry Fielding, Peckinpah's regular composer, abhorred. Another two tracks on the album were alternate renderings of "Billy." Some of the score happily employed guitarist Bruce Langhorne, a longtime Dylan accomplice, whose light touch makes the music shimmer like desert hills in twilight.

"Knockin' On Heaven's Door," which became a top-20 single and attained an eternal life of its own after the picture died at the box office, would stand as the ultimate hymn of the violent Old West. It was heard under a sequence in which the backwater sheriff played by Slim Pickens, mortally gut-shot, staggers to the banks of a river on which his unfinished boat will never sail, trailed by his grieving wife. It's a staggering moment. (Don't seek it in Peckinpah's own cut of the film, however: In the preview version of *PG&BTK*, unearthed in 1988 and now common on DVD, the director – who evidently had second thoughts about Dylan's music – opted to use only the choral introduction of the song, and the rest of the somber ballad was left on the cutting room floor. A bad call.) "Billy," the main musical motif in the film, lyrically cleaves to the plot in outlaw's-eye-view fashion; Dylan's Kid is more sentimentalized and sympathetic than Peckinpah's, who, for all his heroic stature in Kris Kristofferson's rendering, is little better than a bushwhacker. More than one of his filmic victims is plugged in the back.

There may have been precious little real Dylan music to be heard, but at least ticket-buyers got to see him acting on the big screen for the first time (as opposed to playing "Bob Dylan," as he had in *Dont Look Back*). It's hard to tell how much writer Rudy Wurlitzer tailored the part for the neophyte thespian, but Alias – another Man With No Name, even though he's in the wrong movie – is a suitable role for Dylan, and a perfect fit: elfin yet deadly, terse, spookily funny, impassive and ultimately inscrutable. Keaton with a keen-edged Bowie knife. The mask is ideal for him, though the character moves through the action without logic. How does a printer at a small town newspaper become a skilled killer overnight and befriend the territory's most notorious and homicidal outlaw? No matter. With the exception of a couple of awkward scenes near the end of the film, the outsider Dylan dovetails pleasingly with Peckinpah's supporting platoon of greasy, malformed character actors. And he neatly upstages James Coburn's Garrett in a scene in which he does nothing more than read the labels on some tin cans.

Pat Garrett and Billy the Kid passed me by when it came out in 1973. I didn't go to the movies much then. My own guns were nearly in the ground. I was spending most of my time pasted to a barstool at Sterch's on Lincoln Avenue in Chicago, playing "Just Like a Woman" on the jukebox and drinking most nights away with a red-haired woman who would soon leave me, only to reappear two years later in the grooves of a long-playing record. By Bob Dylan, of course.

Released July 13, 1973

"Main Title Theme (Billy)"
"Cantina Theme (Workin' For the Law)"
"Billy 1"
"Bunkhouse Theme"
"River Theme"
"Turkey Chase"
"Knockin' On Heaven's Door"
"Final Theme"
"Billy 4"
"Billy 7"

Dylan

This was a fit of corporate pique, impure product pimped by Columbia Records after David Geffen lured its star into his Asylum with the fattest deal then conceivable. There had been instances of an artist putting together a shitty record to escape a contract, but instances of a major record company putting together a shitty record after its artist had escaped in the name of vengeance were rare indeed. Dylan had been bootlegged by his own label, with evil intent.

Probably conceived on a dartboard after a three-martini lunch, *Dylan* was an exercise in brand devaluation that culled the dregs of its namesake's veering 1969-70 explorations of the American songbook, already plumbed on the excruciating but nonetheless bestselling *Self Portrait*. The nine songs that made up its chintzy 33-minute running time had been steeping for years in the cold brine at the bottom of a warped barrel.

The tracks are distinguished by a truly ugly studio sound (cf. "Sarah Jane" for the nadir) and the worst use of backup vocalists since Anita Kerr joined the sewing bee. The choice of material is inexplicable: There is nothing appetizing about hearing a man of Dylan's vocal gifts covering "Can't Help Falling in Love," or for that matter "Mr. Bojangles." The only moment of interest comes in Dylan's devilish decision to eliminate the titular cab of Joni Mitchell's "Big Yellow Taxi" and replace it with a dumptruck.

In one of those commercial aberrations native to the record business, *Dylan* sold half a million copies and reached the top 20, without a single to support it and despite universally scathing reviews.

Out of loyalty, I refused to either purchase it or listen to it when it came out in 1973. (My thinking was, "Shit, there's always Mott the Hoople.") I heard it for the first time after I bought

The Complete Album Collection Vol. 1. I had missed nothing; it is still atrocious, and an affront.

Released November 16, 1973

"Lily of the West"
"Can't Help Falling in Love"
"Sarah Jane"
"The Ballad of Ira Hayes"
"Mr. Bojangles"
"Mary Ann"
"Big Yellow Taxi"
"A Fool Such As I"
"Spanish is the Loving Tongue"

Planet Waves

How could this not have been a disappointment to some degree? Expectations were so insanely high that they could never be completely met.

Planet Waves may have been the first real "event album" of its day. Dylan hadn't released a collection of new songs in more than three years – *New Morning* had come out in late 1970, and, while his profile was in some eclipse, he still loomed over the musical firmament. Moreover, the record reunited him with the backup musicians of his furious 1966 tour, now known as the Band and standalone stars on their own. That made for a crowded marquee, and the star power was an instant lure; it became Dylan's first No. 1 album in a 12-year career, and the Band's first No. 1 as well. I ran down to a record store on Clark Street and grabbed it the day it came out.

What did we get? A Bob Dylan album, with a glittering, under-rehearsed backup band. It would have been nice if the project had been a true collaborative effort, with songs like "Tears of Rage" and "This Wheel's On Fire," which had been co-authored by Dylan and members of his crew (and recorded by the Band on *Music From Big Pink*). Instead, the Band was relegated to their old role, and not given much time to prep for the sessions. Most of the tracks on the LP were first takes, and it shows: the group's playing is often tentative and sometimes plodding, and stumbles were not ameliorated by a second pass. On their first two albums and to a lesser degree thereafter, the Band had produced meticulous, detailed music, but Dylan's first-take-Charlie modus operandi did not play to their strengths.

Not surprisingly, the best performances are the most unadorned, for the album's best songs are the most naked ones. Dylan's marriage was coming apart in that hour, and he responded with a couple of tunes that were by turns self-lacerat-ing ("Dirge") and surprisingly groveling ("Wedding Song"). Both were cut in separate sessions; just Robbie Robertson's guitar em-bellishes the doom-laden chords of Dylan's piano on the former, while the latter, an eviscerating plea couched as a devotional love song, was played solo. The deepest stuff on *Planet Waves*, they would never be heard in a concert setting. I was personally well situated to appreciate them, and they filled me with discomfort.

The rest, while not bereft of pleasure, was difficult to love without qualification or even to admire deeply. "On a Night Like This" remains a bouncy, engaging invitation, "Going Going Gone" is a wracked confession that sports solid backing by the Band (especially Robbie Robertson, whose playing quivers with dark feeling), and the trifecta of "Tough Mama," "Hazel," and "Something There Is About You" are effective professions of lust and adoration. "You Angel You" never struck me as more than a trifle. "Never Say Goodbye" has always glanced off my ear without affect; I never remember the song is on the album until I hear it playing.

And now I must address My "Forever Young" Problem. The song has proven to be one of Bob's sturdiest copyrights, per-fect for weddings, bar mitzvahs, and funerals, covered to death and beyond, but it has always made my stomach churn. Overripe with bald sentiment, it is obvious in a way that even Dylan's least engaging songs to that point had never been, and its obviousness is glaring in the context of the album's heaviest, more subtly constructed compositions. Worse, it was served up to us *twice* on *Planet Waves*, as a lugubrious ballad and a bounding dance tune. It worked no better with a backbeat than it did as a heart-tugger. In its original long-playing incarnation, the album concluded its first side and began its second side with it; it was a very effective impediment to repeated listening.

So it was a mixed bag at best, and one I continue to grapple with to this day. By the time of its release, on Jan. 17, 1974, my reaction to the album had already been tempered even more by another event: Two weeks before *Planet Waves* came out, I had seen Bob Dylan in concert for the first time, backed by the Band, on the second date of what became the most celebrated tour of its era. And it was quite a show.

Released January 17, 1974

"On a Night Like This"
"Going, Going, Gone"
"Tough Mama"
"Hazel"
"Something There Is About You"
"Forever Young"
"Forever Young"
"Dirge"
"You Angel You"
"Never Say Goodbye"
"Wedding Song"

Before the Flood

E veryone wanted a ticket to the Big Show. I did, too.
  Bob Dylan was kicking off his 1974 U.S. tour – his
first trek in eight years, which had seen him perform a
full set only once, at the Isle of Wight Festival in 1969 – with
two concerts in my hometown, at the old Chicago Stadium on
Madison Avenue. And the Band – the Hawks of old – would be
backing him, as they had in '66, before they had achieved inde-
pendent fame. (I had seen them on their own in Wisconsin, in
1970, and they were thrilling.) Who wouldn't want to see that?
Never much of a concertgoer in my teens and early 20s, I was
jumping for joy at such a rare opportunity.

I was still living in Chicago, in my studio apartment on
Lincoln Avenue, newly solo, working a miserable corporate PR
job at Zenith Radio Corporation on the far west side. Depressed
and alone, I knew the event would dispel at least some of my
gloom. In an unusual move, tickets for the tour were being sold
in a lottery, and I dutifully sent in a check to cover the price of
two $9.50 seats. ($9.50!)

My check was returned (as were those of about 4.9 million
other unlucky aspirants across the country), with a short note
signifying that I had lost the lottery. I was morosely drinking a
beer at my Lincoln Avenue watering hole Sterch's not long thereafter when my friend Marc walked in. Staring into my glass, I informed him of my dismal luck. His face brightened, and he said,
"Hey, I thought I was supposed to get them." And he drew a pair
of tickets to Dylan's second-night show from his jacket pocket
and handed me one. I believe I may have kissed him.

A few weeks later, we regrouped at the bar, where we quaffed
a few drinks. Then Marc handed me the party favor for the night:
a small, square hit of blotter acid, which I chewed and washed

down with a swig of Guinness. We stepped out into the brisk
January air and caught a cab to the Stadium.

By the time we reached the old barn, then the home of
Blackhawks hockey and Bulls basketball, the LSD was starting
to course through our systems. While I had already had some
psychedelic experiences of the wow-I'm-seeing-God variety, this
was a significantly mellower trip. Everything seemed heightened,
in distinctly sharp focus; there were no gaudy hallucinations, but
instead a skyrocketing sense of acute awareness. Though just
18,000 were at the show that night, it felt as if millions were in attendance, and getting to our seats in the loge through the swarm
presented challenges worthy of an Everest climb. Though I can't
remember anything about our stop at the concession stand for
some food, I do recall that we both thought it was hilarious.

Our seats afforded us an unobstructed view of the stage,
which was decorated as if someone was living there, with a com-
fy-looking old sofa and a lamp. There may have been a rug, too.
Or did I dream it? At any rate, the ancient venue felt like home
for a couple of hours.

Thanks to the double-billing, there was no opening act, and
an immense roar went up as Dylan and the Band strode con-
fidently on stage. Dylan was there to rip, and launched into a
fire-spitting rendition of a song I would later learn was "Hero
Blues," an unreleased composition dating back to the early '60s:

When I'm dead
No more good times will I crave
You can stand and shout hero
All over my lonesome grave

Dylan sang the song in a steely yell, pushing to the top of
his register, and all his performances that night were pitched at
a similarly high emotional altitude. The Band was tight and hot,
Robbie Robertson playing with a sting in his tail, Levon Helm
cracking the whip, Rick Danko and Richard Manuel stoking the

bottom, and Garth Hudson creating delicate little cartoons in the air (yes, the drugs had taken hold) with his ornate organ and synthesizer fills. Under the lights the stage seemed to undulate like molten gold.

Since I was obviously *non compos mentis* at the time, I must necessarily reconstruct the evening from an incomplete and possibly not entirely reliable setlist. The night's entertainment comprised several joint Dylan-Band performances, which included a handful of songs from the imminent *Planet Waves*; several Band numbers sans Dylan, including a raucous "Up On Cripple Creek" that implanted itself in the memory; and a few Dylan solo numbers. Of the latter, "It's All Right, Ma (I'm Only Bleeding")" drew the biggest roar: Richard Nixon, in mid-crisis then and undoubtedly loathed by the majority of those in attendance, was on his way out the door, and, even as Dylan sang in his decade-old lyrics, the President of the United States was in fact standing naked. Sometime during the show there was an intermission, but Marc and I were too emulsified to stand, let alone walk around.

One moment is emblazoned in my mind. At the end of the formal show, a cheer, almost a wail, went up. Descriptions of the opening-night date had already circulated; in a then-novel show of appreciation, the audience had responded by lighting matches and holding lighters aloft. The second-night crowd acted in kind, and as pinpoints of light began to flicker in the darkness of our section and spread through the big hall, my elevated senses were illuminated; a brilliant gleam flooded my eyes, and I could swear that the temperature in the building climbed by 100 degrees. That's what I remember best: the light and heat of that moment.

Five months later, Asylum rushed out *Before the Flood*, the authorized record of the '74 tour. With variations, the album replicated the show I had attended. Recorded mostly at dates in Los Angeles, the two-LP package bore a cover shot of matches held aloft in tribute. I listened to the set, a souvenir really, with satisfaction, but also with the knowledge that what was in the sleeve could never quite equal what had been in my head and my heart at the Chicago Stadium.

Released June 20, 1974

"Most Likely You Go Your Way (And I'll Go Mine)"
"Lay Lady Lay"
"Rainy Day Women #12 & 35"
"Knockin' On Heaven's Door"
"It Ain't Me Babe"
"Ballad of a Thin Man"
"Up On Cripple Creek"
"I Shall Be Released"
"Endless Highway"
"The Night They Drove Old Dixie Down"
"Stage Fright"

"Don't Think Twice, It's All Right"
"Just Like a Woman"
"It's Alright, Ma (I'm Only Bleeding)"
"The Shape I'm In"
"When You Awake"
"The Weight"
"All Along the Watchtower"
"Highway 61 Revisited"
"Like a Rolling Stone"
"Blowin' in the Wind"

Blood On the Tracks

Y ou have already met her, briefly, but here is what little else you need to know.

Her name, Constance, still rings like a bell on my ear. Everyone called her Connie, rightly, for she would prove inconstant in the end. Hair as red as an angry sunset spilled down to her shoulders, and she spoke with a soft Florida drawl. I wrote a poem about the red boots she wore everywhere in winter; I had it that bad. I met her just before I returned to school in 1971, and I was instantly infatuated. We lived together for a year in a wood-paneled one-room apartment near Fraternity Row. After we both graduated, she left me and went to New Orleans, while I returned to Chicago. Finally assenting to my increasingly desperate pleas, she joined me up north, but I wouldn't let her breathe, and she soon left again, for good. One too many mornings. I did not stay on the rails. One night, I drank down a pyramid of 10 Wild Turkey shots and presented myself, raving, at my horrified father's door.

On Aug. 9, 1974, the day Richard Nixon resigned, I walked into my boss' office, threw the eighth revision of a press release about a new TV set onto his desk, said, "Fuck you," and walked out the door. Two weeks later, I walked into the studio at the radio station in Wisconsin where I had worked part-time while I was in school, asked my former college radio buddy, now the program director, if he had any work, and was hired on the spot as a full-time DJ, working the overnight shift.

The following January, I was opening mail at the station and found a new Bob Dylan album in one of the boxes. I quickly pulled the LP out of its sleeve, placed it on the turntable, threw the cue switch, and dropped the needle on it. I did not know what to expect.

Early one mornin' the sun was shinin'
I was layin' in bed
Wonderin' if she'd changed at all
If her hair was still red

That stopped me dead. I listened to the rest of the album in awe, my identification complete. Dylan may have been replaying his life in those songs, but he was recounting my own, in detail, right down to the hue of my lost love's hair. Listening to it even now, I find myself living within those songs. I am sure I am not alone in this regard. The world embraced that record, and *Blood On the Tracks*, Dylan's return to Columbia Records, became Bob Dylan's second U.S. No. 1. People heard it in a very special way.

Undoubtedly inspired to a large extent by the gory dissolution of Dylan's eight-year marriage, *Blood On the Tracks* is a record about being torn apart in love, and also about trying to recapture some of what was true and some of what was elusive in that love. It's a ganglion of exposed nerves. Intensely personal yet truly universal in its scope, it ranges through the full spectrum of romance, filled with sorrow, rage, perplexity, bliss, dislocation, fleeting joy, and persistent hope. Dylan stops and gazes long at every signpost on a long and circuitous emotional road. In "You're a Big Girl Now," he quotes a phrase from Marcel Carné's romantic spectacle *Children of Paradise*: "Love is so simple." He disproves that maxim at every bend.

It was Dylan's most carefully executed and assured album in some time; we would later learn that he had labored on it more mightily than he had on any record since *Blonde On Blonde*. After several sessions with Eric Weissberg's group Deliverance in New York, Dylan was initially satisfied with his work, but he had second thoughts after playing an acetate for his brother David Zimmerman. He decided to postpone release of the album and re-cut several of the completed tracks – a wise decision, considering that people probably would have hurled themselves out of tall windows upon hearing the bare, seared original version.

Setting up camp in a Minneapolis studio with a group of deft local musicians, Dylan revisited his songs and ultimately selected five re-cut tracks for the album, leading to a balanced and less arctic edition of the material. It became a poised and sonically inviting folk-rock opus, lacking the barbed, harder-rocking approach of his '60s records, yet warm even in its most starless aspect.

The Twin Cities players acquitted themselves most nobly on the set's two longest tracks. From its still-startling crash of a kick-off – *"Someone's got it in for me, they're planting stories in the press!"* – "Idiot Wind" is a seething indictment that finally bores its way down to its source; the venom in the way he sings "sweet lady" in the second verse burns into the tune like acid. The band seems to flag a little in the later verses, straining over the course of nearly eight minutes to keep up with a relentless and ever-rising outpouring of bile. One has to look back to "Ballad of a Thin Man" and "Positively Fourth Street" for such scathing condemnation; those songs sound polite in comparison.

On the flip side one finds "Lily, Rosemary and the Jack of Hearts," a nine-minute Western movie for the ears. Typical of Dylan, the reels are slightly shuffled, and maybe a few feet of film have been lopped out in the booth. Certainly the backstory is missing. Whipping by at breathtaking speed, it's a storytelling complement to the more confessional songs: A shape-shifting outlaw (there's Melville's Confidence Man again) rides into town to raid a vault and redress some romantic scores. The set is crowded with archetypes, but Jack never really materializes completely before our eyes/ears, and justly so, for he exists less as a character than as a narrative whirlwind, bedecked in shadow, who rearranges the points on a delicate triangle. (Or is it a rectangle?) By the song's end he has simply vanished, leaving death and disorder in his wake.

"Lily, Rosemary and the Jack of Hearts" was an exception, for the rest of the album, mainly cast in the first person, sprang directly from a heart knotted with pain, but in the end still open.

"Tangled Up in Blue," "Simple Twist of Fate," "Meet Me in the Morning," "If You See Her, Say Hello" – despite their dissimilarities, these songs all flowered out of love's cold ground, which Dylan tramps restlessly like a man determined to find some answers in the past, no matter how many miles he has to cover.

Finally, even the most broken soul can be warmed in a sliver of light: Each side of the original LP ended with a muted address to a new lover, "You're Gonna Make Me Lonesome When You Go" and "Buckets of Rain," the latter of which builds an upbeat finale to the album on the back of a sunny Mississippi John Hurt guitar lick.

That complete and beautifully realized album clawed at my heart every day during that late winter of early '75. I played it incessantly on the air, and almost daily at home. One evening, some hours before my midnight shift at the station began, I attended a concert in downtown Madison, and ran smack into Connie, whom I hadn't seen in a year, in the crowded lobby. After a minute or century of uncomfortable conversation, I fled the theater without hearing a note of music and headed for the nearest bar. On my show that night, I played what probably remains my favorite track from *Blood On the Tracks*; I was drunk, but I did not cry when the mic was open.

So: If you see her, say hello.

(Orlando, Florida, spring 1972)

Released January 17, 1975

"Tangled Up in Blue"
"Simple Twist of Fate"
"You're a Big Girl Now"
"Idiot Wind"
"You're Gonna Make Me Lonesome When You Go"
"Meet Me in the Morning"
"Lily, Rosemary and the Jack of Hearts"
"If You See Her, Say Hello"
"Shelter From the Storm"
"Buckets of Rain"

The Basement Tapes

T his fraudulent product, issued eight years after most of its contents were recorded, is an example of a record label identifying the public's desire for a record and then giving the public what it did not want. (Well, not *all* the public: *The Basement Tapes* rose to No. 7 on the U.S. album chart.) But the time was right to revisit some of Dylan's back pages: He had cut his first No. 1 album and embarked on a sold-out U.S. tour with the Band, and had followed up with *Blood On the Tracks*. So there was an inevitability about this gambit, specious as it was.

Most of the material on *The Basement Tapes* was already known to educated listeners. During 1967, Bob Dylan and his erstwhile backing band had reconvened at Dylan's home and the group's collective living quarters, "Big Pink," in the Saugerties. There, in front of some microphones, they ran down a diverse batch of old songs and toyed with some new Dylan compositions (and a couple he co-wrote with his musicians). It was woodshedding, warm-up work, and the music didn't see the light of day officially.

However, when the Dylan bootleg bonanza began in 1969, the so-called "Basement Tapes" were prominently featured on those bathtub-gin LPs. Many of the tracks had emerged on publishing demos, and some were covered by the Byrds, Manfred Mann, and the Band themselves (on their '68 debut *Music From Big Pink*). The English group Coulson Dean McGuinness Flint had cut half a dozen "Basement Tapes" selections on *Lo and Behold*, their delightful 1972 recital of unreleased Dylan material. A live Dylan-Band version of "The Mighty Quinn" (which Mann had taken to No. 1 in the U.K. and No. 10 in the U.S. in 1968) appeared on the misbegotten *Self Portrait* in 1970.

Sensing that there was gold in those chimerical '67 recordings, Columbia issued an "official" album, *The Basement Tapes*, in

June 1975, a mere five months after the arrival of *Blood On the Tracks*. Though fans dutifully bought the two-LP set, it was a botch in almost every respect.

The upwards of 100 tracks cut by Dylan and the Band would ultimately be released in a comprehensive bootleg, but the Columbia album included only 16 numbers from those informal sessions. Most of the Dylan-penned songs on the set were familiar from cover versions; Dylan and the Band's furry, fascinating explorations of old folk, country, and rock 'n' roll songs remained on the vault shelves. The tracks were heard in muddy monophonic renderings, though most of the original performances were made in primitive but well-defined stereo; thus, incredibly, *The Basement Tapes* is one of the few commercial albums ever issued in a stereo-to-mono mix-down with no accompanying stereo version. Worse, the eight numbers featuring the Band were not recorded in the basement(s) at all, but were later identified (in the Band's own 2005 retrospective *A Musical History*) as studio performances, most of them produced by John Simon in late 1967 and early 1968, following the "Basement Tapes" sessions; by that time, Capitol Records had signed the Band, and would launch them with *Music From Big Pink* in July of '68.

Despite its dishonest construction, *The Basement Tapes* was not unlistenable, with Band tracks like the yowling Levon Helm showcase "Yazoo Street Scandal" especially delicious, but it was not revelatory for the hardcore Dylan fan.

One number did make my jaw drop, though. Near the end of side one, a hitherto unknown tune called "Goin' to Acapulco" rose out of the murk, a pearl dredged up from the depths of the Dylan catalog. The song itself is a question mark, its plot and actual meaning as indistinct as its sound and its lyrics. But the atmosphere of the song was so fraught with sadness and desperation that it captured me as tightly as anything on *Blood On the Tracks*. Dylan sings about "going to have some fun," but it is about anything but that; his pain is palpable in every gnarled note he sings. I played it regularly on my radio show, in the hours after midnight, when the blues gripped tightest. I still cherish it today.

Released June 26, 1975

"Odds and Ends"
"Orange Juice Blues (Blues For Breakfast)"
"Million Dollar Bash"
"Yazoo Street Scandal"
"Goin' to Acapulco"
"Katie's Been Gone"
"Lo and Behold!"
"Bessie Smith"
"Clothes Line Saga"
"Apple Suckling Tree"
"Please Mrs. Henry"
"Tears of Rage"
"Too Much of Nothing"
"Yea! Heavy and a Bottle of Bread"
"Ain't No More Cane"
"Crash on the Levee (Down in the Flood)"
"Ruben Remus"
"Tiny Montgomery"
"You Ain't Goin' Nowhere"
"Don't Ya Tell Henry"
"Nothing Was Delivered"
"Open the Door, Homer"
"Long Distance Operator"
"This Wheel's On Fire"

Desire

I was still spinning records in the wilds of Wisconsin when *Desire* was released in early 1976, just slightly less than a year after *Blood On the Tracks* had arrived. It was a rumpled, perplexing record, nowhere near as carefully shaped or consistent in content and tone as its predecessor. But it quickly shot to No. 1 on the album chart; Bob Dylan was coming off his most popular and widely lauded record in years, and his circus-like, star-infested Rolling Thunder Review tour had swept through the East, trailed by a caravan of journalists.

Dylan was news, and we were professionally obliged to play his latest. It was not an easy one to program, even at a free-form FM rock station where "anything goes" was the mantra.

For the first time, Dylan had taken a songwriting partner: Jacques Levy, a New York theater director best known for the 1969 nude revue *Oh Calcutta!*, and a writing collaborator with the Byrds' Roger McGuinn. Levy and Dylan co-authored all but two of the nine tracks on *Desire*, and the results seemed misshapen and awkward.

The songs were recorded by a rag-tag group of little-known musicians Dylan had recruited while making his rounds in the New York clubs; violinist Scarlet Rivera had literally been accosted on the street. The best-known names were his back-up vocalists, Emmylou Harris (then still establishing herself as a soloist following her stint with Gram Parsons) and Ronee Blakely (who would shortly receive an Oscar nomination for her work in Robert Altman's film *Nashville*).

In terms of subject matter and construction, the album's longest tracks harkened back to earlier times. Dylan had gotten interested in the case of Rubin "Hurricane" Carter, a middleweight boxer who had been convicted in a 1966 triple homicide, and he

and Levy wrote an eight-and-a-half minute jeremiad that led off
the LP's first side. Anyone who recalled "The Lonesome Death
of Hattie Carroll" or knew about "Who Killed Davy Moore?"
was unsurprised by the arrival of a new topical Dylan song. But,
while the swirl of Rivera's fiddle kept "Hurricane" from cap-
sizing, it wasn't a number you wanted to listen to frequently. Its
tone was snarling and bluntly didactic, its language sometimes
stilted and inauthentic, and its rushed narrative unfocused and
even confusing. Plus, its extreme length and use of the words
"shit" and "nigger" ensured that it would never be played uned-
ited. It was written for the salon, not the airwaves. It succeeded
in keeping Carter's case in justice's sights, and the fighter was
finally exonerated and freed in 1985. As music, it survives as a
period piece.

Likewise, the 11-minute "Joey" reached back to "John
Wesley Harding," but instead of an Old West gunslinger, its
heroically cast outlaw protagonist was the titular "Crazy" Joey
Gallo, a celebrity mobster who had been snuffed in a 1972 hit
in a Manhattan clam house. Its pileup of admiring detail about
Gallo's style, intelligence, and purported Robin Hood-like be-
nevolence never rings true, and the sluggish flatness and bogus
sentimentality of its drawn-out execution never invites the listener into the story.

Some tracks on the album were handsome enough to command repeated play: the doom-laden, gnomic "One More Cup
of Coffee," the seductive "Oh, Sister," and another outlaw
ballad, "Romance in Durango," with a plot worthy of Marty
Robbins and an offhand reference to Sam Peckinpah (whose
Pat Garrett and Billy the Kid, Dylan's dramatic debut, had been
filmed, chaotically, in Durango, Mexico). "Isis" was in a class by
itself. Its plotline, graced with dark mirth and worthy of Joseph
Campbell's admiration, recounted the tale of a callow youth
who abandons his new bride, embarks on a pointless quest,
and returns remade to the woman he loves. It's one of the few
points on the album where Dylan appears to be having fun, and

it's the lone composition on the record that has maintained its artistic traction.

The other material seemed merely pointless. The lovey-dovey travel poster "Mozambique" couldn't have been more poorly timed: The titular "magical land" in East Africa would soon be scourged by 15 years of civil war, no doubt a blow to tourism. And I still wonder why "Black Diamond Bay" was written and recorded at all – its incomprehensible story, suggested by Joseph Conrad, virtually begged the listener to lift the needle off the album.

Desire ended with the most blatantly autobiographical and cringe-worthy entry in the Dylan discography: "Sara," another plea that made *Planet Waves'* desperate "Wedding Song" sound insouciant by comparison. Dylan replays his marriage, still in tatters, like a man with an old photo album in his hands: "See, we were happy once. Come back." The song was written for an audience of one, and it worked for a while, so it probably doesn't matter that I shudder every time I hear him sing, "Sara, oh Sara, glamorous nymph with an arrow and bow."

It was a wearying thing, this album, and coming on the heels of *Blood On the Tracks*, which probably meant more to me personally than anything I'd ever heard, it put me in a funk.

I was hearing other voices. I'd seen the Wailers in Chicago, and I was more enamored of Bob Marley than of Bob Dylan then. And around this time, a 45, an unusual remake of "Hey Joe," by a young poet and aspiring rocker on the New York scene, belatedly found its way into the studio. (I later learned that Dylan had met her and asked her to join his Rolling Thunder jaunt, but she declined.) I was astonished, and my compass, re-magnetized, began to point in another direction.

Released January 16, 1976

"Hurricane"
"Isis"
"Mozambique"
"One More Cup of Coffee (Valley Below)"
"Oh, Sister"
"Joey"
"Romance in Durango"
"Black Diamond Bay"
"Sara"

Hard Rain

*H*ard Rain was as near as many people got to the Rolling Thunder Revue, Dylan's widely covered tour of 1975-76. A date in a hotel ballroom in Clearwater, Florida – not far from St. Petersburg, hometown of My Red-Haired Lady of *Blood On the Tracks* – was shot as a TV special, then scrapped; a later gig, filmed and recorded in Fort Collins, Colorado a month later, was ultimately shown on NBC. A "soundtrack album," drawn from the latter show and one in Texas, was issued in September 1976.

I watched the telecast when it aired. Shot under wet, grey skies on the next-to-last Revue stop, it was a largely cheerless affair. Save the faithful Joan Baez and Ramblin' Jack Elliott, all of the original co-stars and the platoon of celebrity hangers-on had departed the tour by May of '76; on the TV show, Baez dueted briefly, while Elliott lurked at the back of the stage, unutilized. For his part, Dylan, sans whiteface and the other commedia trappings he had affected in '75, appeared angry, possibly because he had to carry the entire enterprise on his narrow shoulders again. It was dispiriting viewing. Dylan and his circus caravan had reached the end of the road; the ground was too muddy to sink the tentpoles.

On record, it's a curiosity. As many as five guitars are employed; there is a lot of bellowing back-up singing; Scarlet Rivera's violin, the most interesting instrumental fillip in Dylan's music of the era, has been pushed into the background. The rhythm section of bassist Rob Stoner and drummer Howie Wyeth raises some sand on the rockers, especially on a rousing version of "Shelter From the Storm." However, as an ensemble, the lurching, overstuffed band is incapable of playing much interesting music at slow tempos. Plus, Dylan's lyrical revisions and additions to "Lay Lady Lay" (embarrassing) and "One Too Many Mornings" (pointless) add nothing.

That was as close as I got to the Revue. The tour never pulled within several hundred miles of Madison, and I was financially ill-equipped to travel in those days. I'd dutifully read accounts of the jaunt by the playwright Sam Shepard and Larry "Ratso" Sloman, the latter of whom was briefly a colleague and comrade-in-arms at the University of Wisconsin's campus paper.

I was not done with Rolling Thunder, though. In the spring of 1977 — after being unceremoniously asked for my keys to the studio by my program director on the eve of a week-long vaca-tion in California — I moved to Los Angeles. I had been hired as the in-house publicist and scribe for a chain of repertory and art movie houses.

One of my early tasks was to assist on local publicity for our opening of *Renaldo & Clara*, the four-hour movie shot during the Revue tour and arduously completed in the ensuing two years. Scenes from concerts shot in the early, colorful, luminary-filled 1975 shows were intercut with unfathomable dramaturgy and copious amateurish improvisation, all "written" and "directed" by Dylan without any attention to coherence. Sara Dylan co-starred; by the time the film opened in January 1978, the couple had been divorced for six months.

It was like *Children of Paradise* as shot by John Cassavetes during a protracted and extremely destructive bender. To say that the reviews were uncharitable would be generous. The grosses were horrific; at times the movie played to nearly empty houses. My company also handled a hastily edited two-hour cut of *R&C* that was no better and performed no more lucratively than the original. Neither version has officially escaped the vaults since.

I was stupefied by the picture, but at least I managed to remain conscious for its interminable length. At the first, pri-vate screening I attended, I found myself seated next to Kris Kristofferson. Within an hour, he was fast asleep. Fortunately he did not snore loudly.

Released September 10, 1976

"Maggie's Farm"
"One Too Many Mornings"
"Stuck Inside of Mobile With the Memphis Blues Again"
"Oh, Sister"
"Lay Lady Lay"
"Shelter From the Storm"
"You're a Big Girl Now"
"I Threw It All Away"
"Idiot Wind"

Street-Legal

U ntil the release of *Street-Legal* in 1978, no Bob Dylan studio album aroused anything resembling ambivalence. There were records to love and records to hate; even the stuff that hovered in between, like *Desire*, could command some sort of passion, or at least attention. But *Street-Legal*, recorded in the midst of a year-long tour, was a *m'eh* album before albums were *m'eh*. Not good enough to be loved, not bad enough to be loathed, it was a record that just sort of sat around, as it did in my Westwood apartment after I bought it. With each passing day, it moved further back in a stack of newly purchased LPs that leaned against my bedroom wall. I doubt that I played it more than three times, for there was more exciting stuff to hear.

I'll speak of the good stuff first, since I know there are some who would maintain that nothing is very good about it. "New Pony" is a strong, slavering blues; "Baby, Stop Crying" is a nice love song with a hook that commands your attention; and the album's wrenching final track, "Where Are You Tonight? (Journey Through Dark Heat)," though scarred somewhat by its mock-Al Kooper organ line, is an agonized post-divorce labor of loss that cuts way deeper than anything preceding it. Three for nine: more than respectable for baseball, not so much for long-playing albums.

The remainder of the record was torpedoed by its murky sound and murkier lyrics. The incessant and obtrusive chirping of Dylan's background singers squeezes the air out of virtually every song; the band, comprising Rolling Thunder vets and new recruits, is studio-competent and completely unexciting; and Dylan himself sounds distressingly disengaged on the majority of the tracks.

One can hear something brewing here: The album is dotted with scriptural references (cf. "Changing of the Guards" and "Señor"), the back-up vocalists lend a gospel feel to the proceedings, and there's an atmosphere of unease, the sense of a chapter closing.

It abides as source material for a compilation many have probably made: *Decent Songs From So-So and Lousy Bob Dylan Albums.*

Released June 15, 1978

"Changing of the Guards"
"New Pony"
"No Time to Think"
"Baby Stop Crying"
"Is Your Love in Vain?"
"Señor (Tales of Yankee Power)"
"True Love Tends to Forget"
"We Better Talk This Over"
"Where Are You Tonight (Journey Through Dark Heat)"

Bob Dylan at Budokan

I bought this fucking thing as an import at Tower Records in Westwood, and when Columbia belatedly released it at a domestic price I felt seriously ripped off.

Bob Dylan at Budokan was its author's third live album in four years. Though its release post-dated that of *Street-Legal*, it was actually recorded at the Tokyo venue in early 1978, two months before that studio album was recorded and four months before it reached stores. Dylan spent 114 days on the road that year, touring the Far East, Europe, and the U.S. The Budokan shows from which the live package was drawn took place near the trek's beginning. The two-LP set was issued at first for the Japanese market, but widespread importing led Columbia to release it in the U.S. in April 1979.

This inferior, often glitzy recital of familiar tunes, some of them drastically and appallingly reconfigured, filled me with misery; it was such an effort to put it on the turntable that it felt like it weighed a ton. In fact, listening to it literally became *work*.

In October 1978, I was enlisted as the freelance "rock critic" for the *Los Angeles Reader*, an alternative weekly launched by the Chicago paper of the same name. Some years before, I'd had a music column in a Midwestern underground paper, and I was serving as L.A. correspondent for a short-lived Madison music weekly, so I knew the drill, and I wanted an L.A. outlet for my writing. My friend Myron Meisel, the *Reader*'s film critic, recommended me for the gig at the new paper, and I would hold it – except for a year off during the tenure of an especially insane publisher – for the next 18 years, from the rag's first issue to its last.

I was given complete liberty to write about whatever I wanted to. I wouldn't have had it any other way, since the *Reader* initially paid me a princely $25 for a 1,500-word piece. By then I was utterly involved in the punk rock scene in L.A., and many of my pieces surveyed punk of both the homegrown and foreign varieties. But I would still return to the music of artists from an earlier era whose work meant something to me, and Dylan was a constant during those years. But my musical consciousness had changed, and I was not inclined to be forgiving.

As it was then, playing *Bob Dylan at Budokan* today is an enervating experience. My opinion of the record hasn't altered perceptibly, so I'll quote from my original review, published in the Feb. 9, 1979, edition of the *Reader* and recently exhumed from a Public Storage box:

"...The unwieldy, bloated arrangements don't merely frame the songs, they memorialize them. Three female backup singers stridently punctuate Dylan's vocals with useless reiterative emphasis.

"The individual musicians seem straightjacketed by the stiff-backed arranging. Guitarist Billy Cross contributes many needlessly busy solos and fills. [Saxophonist] Steve Douglas, the unsung hero of a hundred Phil Spector singles, plays the same solo over and over again with nightmarish regularity. Each tune smashes along like a juggernaut, with a mind-dulling sameness; the heaviness of the whole affair defies start-to-finish listening.

"The Budokan performances introduce an element new to Dylan's music: kitsch. The version of 'Love Minus Zero/No Limit' here features a lilting flute right out of Crispian St. Peters' junky '60s hit 'The Pied Piper.' The new arrangement of 'All I Really Want to Do' threatens to break into 'The 59th Street Bridge Song' at any moment...

"A true signpost of creative poverty during the '70s has been the reggae adaptation of a previously recorded song. California artists are the most consistent offenders in this area of musical crime, but at Budokan, Dylan jumped on the bandwagon, apparently spurred on by too much time spent in Malibu. There are not one but two reworkings on the album: a flaccid reading of 'Knockin' On Heaven's Door' that doesn't approach the power of similar performances by Television or even Eric Clapton, and a ludicrous, thumping parody of 'Don't Think Twice, It's Alright.'"

It went on like this for a while. I even offered a comparison to Elvis Presley of the Later Jumpsuit Years, for Dylan's gaudy wardrobe and flaccid attack of the period made such a juxtaposition an easy shot. I nonetheless gave my blessing to a handful of the album's 22 tracks – "Shelter From the Storm" was an especially sturdy vehicle — and suggested that Dylan might still be capable of making another great record.

At the time, this album played like the work of a man who had forgotten what his own music was about.

Released in Japan November 22, 1978

"Mr. Tambourine Man"
"Shelter From the Storm"
"Love Minus Zero/No Limit"
"Ballad of a Thin Man"
"Don't Think Twice, It's All Right"
"Maggie's Farm"
"One More Cup of Coffee (Valley Below)"
"Like a Rolling Stone"
"I Shall Be Released"
"Is Your Love in Vain?"
"Going, Going, Gone"

"Blowin' in the Wind"
"Just Like a Woman"
"Oh, Sister"
"Simple Twist of Fate"
"All Along the Watchtower"
"I Want You"
"All I Really Want to Do"

"Knockin' On Heaven's Door"
"It's Alright, Ma (I'm Only Bleeding)
"Forever Young"
"The Times They Are a-Changin'"

Slow Train Coming

There he was, the man who told us you don't need a weath-
erman to know which way the wind blows, wearing his
Witness News blazer, giving us the forecast: "Tomorrow
it'll be fiery, with a 90% chance of brimstone."

At the time *Slow Train Coming* arrived in 1979, I was a thor-
oughgoing agnostic. I certainly had no God I could call my own.
My mother's family was (non-observing) Greek Orthodox, my father's (non-observing) Jewish. On Sunday mornings, I had stayed
at home and read the *New York Times*. The only meaningful thing
that had ever happened to me in a house of worship up was
seeing *Citizen Kane* for the first time at the Unitarian Church in
Evanston, Illinois, when I was 16. In '79 I was living a completely
heathen and hedonistic lifestyle. I was not favorably inclined to
religion as any sort of answer to my existential questions.

So I thus did not welcome Bob Dylan's wholehearted conversion to evangelical Christianity, which was the subject matter of
his album. In fact, I suppose you could say I was a little enraged.

It was not so much that Dylan, raised in a Jewish family, had
embraced Jesus Christ as his Lord and Savior. I could honor the
choice – it was his, not mine. He may have been headed down
that road for some time: His liner notes to *Highway 61 Revisited*
concluded with a reference to the "holy slow train." But the variety of Christianity to which he subscribed filled me with unease.
Dylan's brand of belief – the product of experiencing a Christian
epiphany on a stage in San Diego and his subsequent associa-
tion with the Vineyard Fellowship, an L.A. evangelical church to
which the musician's girlfriend had introduced him – was a take-
it-or-leave-it proposition, and I was unwilling to take it. It felt
narrow (and, by Dylan's own definition, it was), self-righteous,
unloving, wrathful and almost entirely humorless – a "my way or

the highway" type of faith. And I resented the music he was using as his pulpit. He was writing a new kind of "finger-pointing
song," and he was sticking that "one way" finger right in my eye.
I extended another finger in kind.

The ideology came packaged attractively. *Slow Train Coming*
was produced by Jerry Wexler (an atheist!) and Barry Beckett at
Muscle Shoals Sound in Alabama, and it was, sonically speaking, his most listenable album in some years. The backup singers
were held in check for once, ironically enough, and the ersatz
Albert King of Mark Knopfler was not an unattractive lead instrumental voice. The songs were melodic and carefully crafted,
and there were even some nice, engaging grooves. Dylan's singing was quite subtle and nuanced. But the record emptied my
heart and depressed me.

The album prompted a lot of head-scratching, confusion,
and bile among fellow Dylan fans I knew. However, some, including colleagues in the alternative press, championed the new
music, and even suggested that it was me, and not Dylan, who
was narrow-minded for not cheering it on. There were a few
who got a bit exercised in its defense. I recall running into Bob
Hilburn, then the pop music critic for the *Los Angeles Times*,
at a gig at the Whisky. Our conversation turned to *Slow Train
Coming*, which I had recently panned in the *LA Reader*. As our
debate escalated, Hilburn – one of the most sweet-tempered and
open-minded guys I've ever known, but also a man inclined to
celebrate Dylan with unquestioning ardor – actually grabbed me
by the front of my jacket as he made a case for the record. In the
end, I said to Bob, "I ain't buyin'," or words to that effect, and
headed for the bar.

Maybe I just wanted to pop off another shot at him, but
I decided to attend one of Dylan's dates at the Santa Monica
Civic in November 1979. My worst nightmares were realized.
Walking up to the hall, I was greeted by glassy-eyed throngs of
born-again believers, some wearing t-shirts emblazoned with the
legend "HALLELUJAH," hoisting signs with New Testament

citations and literally waving Bibles. Inside, the Civic was deathly still – not even a note of traditional gospel to warm the night. Pastor Bob took the stage clad in what I would later describe as "Church of Las Vegas" garb. Dylan and his flock played a workmanlike and unexciting set of material from *Slow Train Coming* and some unrecorded numbers in the same mode. Some in the crowd who looked like they could not be counted among long-time Dylan enthusiasts danced, and cheered when the proselytizing star offered such between-song homilies as, "People are so conditioned to bad news, they don't know good news when they hear it." I finally fled, moving toward the door through a growing number of audibly disgruntled audience members in the lobby.

In that time, Dylan drew a line in the sand, and I chose not to cross it. Many did: *Slow Train Coming* became a No. 3 album, and "Gotta Serve Somebody" reached the top 30 and won him his first Grammy. I only heard a man howling hosannas in a creative wilderness he had staked out for himself. His music felt very small to me. Even today, I am unable to listen to the album with any pleasure.

Released August 18, 1979

"Gotta Serve Somebody"
"Precious Angel"
"I Believe in You"
"Slow Train"
"Gonna Change My Way of Thinking"
"Do Right to Me Baby (Do Unto Others)"
"When You Gonna Wake Up"
"Man Gave Names to All the Animals"
"When He Returns"

Saved

I could hardly get past the cover, those hands reaching to Heaven. Neither could a lot of other people, and so Columbia replaced it in 1985.

If you got around to playing the record inside that ugly and horrifyingly schematic jacket, you heard something about as close to a Bob Dylan gospel record as you were going to get. The question was, did you want or need one?

Saved reunited Dylan with the production team of Jerry Wexler and Barry Beckett at Muscle Shoals, but it was made not with the comparatively supple *Slow Train Coming* band, but with Dylan's touring group – not a bad one, merely an overbearing one — which had performed much of the material on the 1979 tour, including the Santa Monica stop I attended. Wexler and Beckett did little more than turn on the tape machine. The sound returned to the bombast of the Budokan recordings. The lyrics – save for the bizarro Christian love song "Covenant Woman" – replayed familiar gospel imagery, minus any compelling spin. Dylan's singing had never sounded harsher, and his earnest attempts at soulfulness did not convince.

I already had zero patience with Dylan's professions of blind faith, and this record was not going to convince me that I was misguided the first time. I listened to *Saved* once and put it aside in disgust. I wondered then if my connection with Dylan's music had reached its terminus.

Yes, I did listen to it again, more than once. Still painful.

Released June 20, 1980

"A Satisfied Mind"
"Saved"

"Covenant Woman"
"What Can I Do For You?"
"Solid Rock"
"Pressing On"
"In the Garden"
"Saving Grace"
"Are You Ready"

Shot of Love

It was a mess, possibly as messy as the inside of Dylan's head when it was written and recorded. But for all that, *Shot of Love*, and the B-side of an attendant 1981 single, offered hope to those like me who were weary of the Evangelical Bob. There was the sound of a door opening; light entered the room through a crack.

Produced by Chuck Plotkin, the record is unquestionably the worst-sounding one Dylan had made up to that point. The drums are so poorly mic'ed that Jim Keltner appears to be playing with his elbows. The studio ambience bruises the ear. On the album's loudest tracks, the performances are distorted and downright abrasive. Confusion and disorder extended to the LP's packaging – God knows what Columbia's marketing department was thinking when they slapped the atrocious faux-Lichtenstein op art cover on the sleeve.

It was still largely a project driven by Dylan's Christian conversion, and its worst songs – two excoriations of the unbelievers, "Property of Jesus" and "Dead Man, Dead Man" – offered the kind of obvious expressions of spiteful contempt that had grown familiar on the preceding two records.

But there were surprises. "In the Summertime" is a love song, simple and cloaked at the same time; the recording of it is terrible, but it has maintained its sweetness, and I have heard an atheist of my acquaintance perform it beautifully. "Lenny Bruce" is not an especially well-written eulogy, but this unexpected homage to the late, publicly pilloried comic and social critic, then dead 14 years, showed that Dylan had more on his mind than pieties.

Two other songs came as a shock to the system. One, "The Groom's Still Waiting at the Altar," was a blaring, hard-rocking number that originally appeared as the flip side of a slight *Shot of Love* track, the lightly reggae-fied "Heart of Mine." I believe I bought it on the recommendation of a clerk at Rhino Records, the Westwood store that was then serving as a kind of living room for me. It was in fact inspired by a Blblical passage, from John's gospel, but its appalled scattergun take on world chaos was bracing in a way none of Dylan's other religious work had been. It dared you not to listen to it. (It was tardily added to *Shot of Love* when the album was re-released as a compact disc.)

Then there was "Every Grain of Sand," the LP's final track. Again, it was drawn from scripture, from a passage in the gospel according to St. Matthew in which Jesus instructs his disciples about their ministry. Could Dylan himself have been thinking about the nature of his own role, as a Christian and as an artist? Certainly, something was moving within him. It's a lovely and subdued piece, humble and inward-looking, yet cosmic in its scope, and the language is breathtaking and deployed with assurance. The welcome restraint of the performance telegraphs every note meaningfully.

Here, Bob Dylan did something perhaps even he himself may not have believed he was capable of: He wrote a great *hymn*, a song big and wide enough that even this skeptic could feel admitted into it and admire it without reservation. It gave me...faith.

Released August 12, 1981

"Shot of Love"
"Heart of Mine"
"Property of Jesus"
"Lenny Bruce"
"Watered-Down Love"
"The Groom's Still Waiting at the Altar"
"Dead Man, Dead Man"
"In the Summertime"
"Trouble"
"Every Grain of Sand"

Infidels

I was prone to be charitable towards *Infidels* when it was re-leased in late 1983. I was newly married, had bought a house, and my work was appearing in *Rolling Stone* and *Musician*. So, like many another writer, I sprinkled some praise in the *Reader* on Dylan's first studio album after two years of near-absolute silence. I can't unearth the piece now, but I'm sure I erred on the positive side, for the record has not aged well.

The dogs of apostasy had torn at Dylan's coat, and *Infidels*, though it still traded on Biblical imagery, seemed a fairly defin-itive break with the evangelical past. His new orientation was telegraphed in a photograph that appeared in September, show-ing him standing at the Wailing Wall in a yarmulke and tallit. The questioning "Jokerman," which commenced the album, arced through spirituality's history with refreshing doubt and welcome lyrical extravagance.

But that opening shot was the most distinguished entry on a record that careened around uncertainly. Nothing about the endeavor hung together. Though Mark Knopfler, the champi-on player on *Slow Train Coming*, returned to the (now-secular) fold, and the lineup included onetime Stones guitarist Mick Taylor and Jamaican reggae rhythm stars Sly Dunbar and Robbie Shakespeare, the performances never coalesced, and were sin-gularly lacking the force one associates with the best of Dylan.

There was purely topical material: "Neighborhood Bully," about Israel's uneasy position in global politics, and "Union Sundown," about the collapse of labor and the exportation of manufacturing, were both bald-faced and transitory in affect, though at least the former was played purposefully. Little bet-ter was "Man of Peace," an excoriation of false prophets. The vague condemnation of "License to Kill" has never borne a keen point, nor has "I and I," couched in its murky Rastafarian patois.

The rueful, baffled "Don't Fall Apart On Me Tonight" isn't without its provocations, but it's freeze-dried forever by its '80s production sound, and it is not well sung, like the rest of the album. Don't ask me what the hell "Sweetheart Like You" is all about. I'm not sure it's worth mustering the brain power to explicate it.

I listened to *Infidels* scrupulously when it came out, and then filed it away for decades. About the only time I would think about it came years later, when a question thrust itself into my head: "Why the hell did Dylan leave 'Blind Willie McTell' off that record?" The mystery abides.

Released November 1, 1983

"Jokerman"
"Sweetheart Like You"
"Neighborhood Bully"
"License to Kill"
"Man of Peace"
"Union Sundown"
"I and I"
"Don't Fall Apart On Me Tonight"

Real Live

I don't think I ever heard *Real Live* on its original release in December 1984. At that time, I was up late most nights, coaxing my infant son Max to sleep in the living room rocking chair. It may have been in the house, but I never got to it. So my assessment of necessity comes about 30 years after the fact.

This record probably would have kept Max awake, or just made him crankier. Recorded in England and Ireland that summer, it was Dylan's stab at a straightforward "rock album," or as straightforward as he could make it. The artillery was heavy enough: The band members included Mick Taylor, back for a tour go-round, and keyboardist Ian McLagan of the Faces, while Carlos Santana dropped in to play a couple forgettable choruses on "Tombstone Blues."

Dylan must have thought stadium rock was the way to go, because he attempts his best Stones impression on the Chuck Berry-inspired "Highway 61 Revisited" and the cranked-up boogie of "Maggie's Farm." As a strategy for a live LP, it falls flat, because the recorded sound is horrifically dull, with Taylor's normally hyper-potent guitar sounding like it's emanating from a car dashboard speaker. Two songs from *Infidels* are clubbed to death. Dylan's vocalizing is mannered in the extreme (see "Ballad of a Thin Man" for the most egregious example), and the album features some of his most preposterous harmonica noodling anywhere.

Three acoustic performances, still *de rigeur* at a Dylan concert, fare no better. "It Ain't Me Babe" and "Girl From the North Country" are merely superfluous, but one has to wonder what possessed Dylan to almost completely rewrite "Tangled Up in Blue" for appearances on this tour. It's ludicrous, silly and affectless. Texts are not sacred, but if you're going to pen a new one, make sure it's better than the original.

Live albums are by definition *product*. In Dylan's case, it doesn't seem to matter what era it is, but the product has almost always been pointless. Some of *Real Live* was cut in Newcastle. You can hear the coal being carried there on this disc.

Released December 3, 1984

"Highway 61 Revisited"
"Maggie's Farm"
"I and I"
"License to Kill"
"It Ain't Me Babe"
"Tangled Up in Blue"
"Masters of War"
"Ballad of a Thin Man"
"Girl From the North Country"
"Tombstone Blues"

Empire Burlesque

Bob Dylan with...syndrums?
Somewhere in an alternative universe there may exist a version of *Empire Burlesque* that I might want to listen to if not forced. The songs are not dishonorable; I find virtue in "Seeing the Real You at Last," "When the Night Comes Falling From the Sky," and "Something's Burning, Baby," all interesting tunes about fucked-up relationships. I also like the anti-military bop of "Clean Cut Kid." Truth be told, I might admire the material here more than most of the stuff on *Infidels*.

Unfortunately, Dylan chose this awkward juncture to attempt a rapprochement with the Sound of Today. He produced the album, so most of the blame for its embarrassing mummified sound can be laid at his feet. The entire project was slathered in a chilly contemporary gloss that was a light year removed from the tradition-based matrix in which Dylan had created his best work. The present was not working for him. It stands as the most dated-sounding of any of his records today. (Of course, '80s records by many another artist may also be likewise condemned.) "When the Night Comes Falling From the Sky" might as well be called "Disco Apocalypse."

I will not castigate Dylan for entrusting the mixing of this misbegotten thing to Arthur Baker, who was then flashing a hot hand among dance and hip-hop producers. Hell, I liked what Baker was up to. His 12-inch extended mix of Springsteen's "Dancing in the Dark" was superior to the original track on *Born in the USA* (speaking of dated), and turned that record's similarly of-the-moment attack into something expansive and exciting. (It should be noted that "Dark Eyes," the acoustic track at the end of the album, and the one that comes closest to being a saving grace, was recorded at Baker's behest.) However, in the case of the Dylan record, he was just repainting a sonic outhouse.

Even in its day, *Empire Burlesque* sounded terrible, a product of confusion, uncertainty, and horrible miscalculation. Like most critics, I dismissed it harshly. It was 1985, the beginning of an arid time for music, and here Dylan was smack in the middle of the desert, marking time in the wasteland amid the Moogs.

Released June 8, 1985

"Tight Connection to My Heart (Has Anybody Seen My Love)"
"Seeing the Real You at Last"
"I'll Remember You"
"Clean Cut Kid"
"Never Gonna Be the Same Again"
"Trust Yourself"
"Emotionally Yours"
"When the Night Comes Falling From the Sky"
"Something's Burning, Baby"
"Dark Eyes"

Knocked Out Loaded

It took a small army of musicians and lots of expensive studio time to concoct this record, which is mainly a bag of rocks. Covers of Little Junior Parker (senseless) and Kris Kristofferson (kiddie chorus: a big no-no), some purloining from Bill Monroe, an airless version of "Precious Memories," another original I can't remember five minutes after I've heard it, and three co-writes, one of them with Carole Bayer Sager. *Carole Bayer Sager.* How's that again?

But one of the co-writes is "Brownsville Girl," authored with playwright-actor Sam Shepard, who went along for the ride on the Rolling Thunder Revue, and recorded and then scrapped in a variant version during sessions for *Empire Burlesque*. The 11-minute tune is as demented as *Duel in the Sun*, one of the Gregory Peck horse operas that Dylan references in this strange, meandering saga. Dense, unpredictable, and frequently hilarious, the song is finally swamped by its grotesque overproduction (though I can't fault any song in which Dylan's customarily aggravating background singers are used for obvious humorous effect). It's a mad Western Odyssey shot in 3D and Cinerama that revels in its own widescreen insanity, "Tangled Up in Blue" at the Bijou on acid. Annoying and entertaining in equal measures, it's the only thing on the album that justifies removing it from its sleeve.

And from my point of view, it didn't hurt that there was another red-haired woman up on Bob's screen.

Released August 8, 1986

"You Wanna Ramble"
"They Killed Him"
"Drifting Too Far From Shore"

"Precious Memories"
"Maybe Someday"
"Brownsville Girl"
"Got My Mind Made Up"
"Under Your Spell"

Down in the Groove

own in the Groove had no real reason to exist. Dylan was
now releasing records reflexively. This excrescence was
probably cobbled together to promote his U.S. summer
tour of 1988. It does not contain a single worthwhile song written by Bob Dylan. Only four of its 10 tracks can be considered
"originals"; two were co-written by Robert Hunter, the Grateful
Dead's lyricist. Better than Carole Bayer Sager, I suppose.

The tunes are all dismal. Had Dylan ever applied his talents
to anything as dreadful as "Ugliest Girl in the World?" I'm pretty sure he had not, though there may be outtakes that are even
worse. It can be said with certainty that this album is worse than
1973's execrable *Dylan*, since Bob himself *actually let the record company release it.*

In truth, I can stand to listen to the covers of Hank Snow's
"Ninety Miles an Hour (Down a Dead End Street)" and the
Stanley Brothers' "Rank Strangers." Bob is here imitating Ry
Cooder (hence the presence of Ry's vocalists Bobby King and
Willie Green on the former track), but credibly, and the singing is
for once legit. However, Bob Dylan should never have to imitate
Ry Cooder.

The musical contributors include Eric Clapton, Ron Wood,
members of the Sex Pistols and the Clash, and Sly and Robbie.
Nobody plays shit.

The running time, 32:05, is a blessing. The album is over before you can summon up the energy to get off the couch, take it
out of the player, and throw it across the room.

That August, enticed by free ducats proffered by a no doubt
desperate record company, and by privileges at the backstage bar,
I went to see Dylan at the Greek Theatre in L.A. He was supported by a trio fronted by G.E. "Guitar Enema" Smith of the

Saturday Night Live band. By maybe the sixth number, I was gone like a cool breeze. Even free liquor was not worth that.

Released May 31, 1988

"Let's Stick Together"
"When Did You Leave Heaven"
"Sally Sue Brown"
"Death is Not the End"
"Had a Dream About You, Baby"
"Ugliest Girl in the World"
"Silvio"
"Ninety Miles An Hour (Down a Dead End Street)"
"Shenandoah"
"Rank Strangers to Me"

Dylan and the Dead

I never hated the Grateful Dead. I loved the early records, and not just because I was on drugs. In fact, the band was responsible for one of the most entertaining shows I ever went to, at the University of Wisconsin Field House in 1971. It was the Pigpen era, and all was still very groovy. It was supposed to be a sit-down concert; the kids in attendance, who were so high they floated into the venue, took one look at the chairs on the floor and hastily folded them up, stacked them in a huge mountain in the middle of the enormous room, and danced a circle around them in ecstasy for two hours.

Therefore, despite my latter-day conversion to punk rock, it was not preordained that I would detest the double bill of Bob Dylan and the Dead that I saw at Anaheim Stadium in July of 1987, even though Bob wasn't exactly on a roll at that point and the Dead's days of making interesting music were at least a decade behind them. They were all born folkies, and there was the possibility they could make simpatico music together.

Three of the seven songs on *Dylan and the Dead* were recorded at the date I attended. The gig was bad, literally laughably bad. It deserved a *Mystery Science Theater 3000*-style commentary. Dylan yelled as the Dead groaned backup vocals and chugged listlessly behind him; with a clause allowing him to wank on at least one number evidently written into his contract, Jerry Garcia obliged with an onanistic solo on "All Along the Watchtower," the standard for Dylan Guitar Overkill since Hendrix placed his magical fingers on the tune. The repertoire was feeble, and there were Christian numbers, too. I can't recall with any certainty who I was with that day, but I know for damn sure that we split early. Premature exits from Dylan shows were becoming habitual.

It was a money gig put together in a lawyer's office. The recorded evidence was damning, excruciatingly accurate, and thoroughly unnecessary, and remains so.

Released February 6, 1989

"Slow Train"
"I Want You"
"Gotta Serve Somebody"
"Queen Jane Approximately"
"Joey"
"All Along the Watchtower"
"Knockin' On Heaven's Door"

Oh Mercy

In the fall of 1989, my wife packed her VW van, gathered up my two young sons, and moved to Flagstaff. It had all been going south for a while, and I had driven it there. I loved my boys, but they didn't keep me at home, for I was crawling out of my own skin. I prowled the city, Hollywood, the West Side, Venice, looking for God knows what, but I know I went about it wrong. A man shouldn't give his address out to bad company, but I had, and so I found myself sitting in a car in East Hollywood, waiting as one of my barroom friends scored his junk. I drank in every hellhole in the city, and they all let me drink until I was blind. One club owner would pull me into the office as soon as I walked in the door and dump a pile of blow on the desk. I wanted someone I knew I shouldn't, and she wanted me, but guilt overtook me, and it went into the ditch. Now I was living alone in a three-bedroom house with a broken gate, leaks in the roof, and a six-pack and a bottle of Stolichnaya in the refrigerator; the weeds on the lawn were as tall as elephant grass. I'd set fire to my life.

I somehow managed to hang onto my sanity and my job, by my fingernails, but my nights grew later and longer. I'd drink at home, and my closest companion during those hours became a new Bob Dylan album. I had no reason to expect that I would ever want such companionship, never dreamed of it actually, for his music had left me profoundly unmoved for many years. But there were countless nights when I turned off all the lights and stretched out on the soiled, lumpy couch and listened to *Oh Mercy* filling the room. I thought of other, brighter days when my candle was burning magnesium-hot at both ends, and "Visions of Johanna" and "Sad Eyed Lady of the Lowlands" had filled the hours approaching dawn. They had vibrated in the room the same way.

It was the sound of the record that drew me in at first. The music didn't seem to emanate from my speakers; it hung in the air like drapes, or like crepe. I was of course drawn to the songs of collapsed love first – "Where Teardrops Fall," "Man in the Long Black Coat," "Most of the Time," "What Was It You Wanted," "What Good Am I?" There was emotion in those deft songs, real longing and regret, confusion, pain! *"Don't even remember what her lips felt like on mine…most of the time."* And the music made that funereal emotion palpable, something you could almost touch with your hand. Daniel Lanois had produced the record (in an antique, atmospheric house in New Orleans, I would learn later), so carefully that a single note would rise out of the mix and pierce me, a steeply ascending bass line would thrust me down a rabbit hole.

Eventually I would connect with the rest of the songs on the record. I could understand the world-chaos that permeated "Political World" and "Everything is Broken," the album's two most rocking songs, though they rolled more than rocked, and rippled too. Yes, certainly, everything was broken. I could identify myself in the bitter condemnation that was "The Disease of Conceit" – I had been sick with it. I accepted the blessing that was "Ring Them Bells," that gathering of saints. And I saw my own life, and the lives of one or two others, arcing by me in "Shooting Star."

Then I had no idea how this album had come to pass, how Dylan had found his way to exactly the same place I was, or at least someplace so much like it that I recognized it immediately, with intensity. I'd experienced something similar with one of his records 15 years before, but I couldn't have anticipated it happening again as I rounded the curve, hollowed out and mad with sorrow, into middle age.

His voice stood out in relief, touched with the scratch of age, sometimes with a simmering rage, sometimes with remorse or disbelief. That effect had something to do with the necromancy of the production; the sound had a hyper-reality to it that I'd never experienced in his music previously. Through the songs or through the sound, *he was in the room with me.* And, listening, I was there with him.

I essayed *Oh Mercy* in print, professionally enough, praising it as many others did. I was hurting, and so I kept some things to myself. For me, its success was not merely about the rebirth of an artist after years off the trail, though the album certainly told that story. My response was not primarily an aesthetic one. The record was a mirror, a glass of water, a beacon, oxygen, a book written by another in which I read myself.

It is one of the handful of records I've ever heard for which I can say I am truly grateful, for it brought some grace into my withered world. In Dylan's canon, and in my life, it occupies a sacred space.

Released September 22, 1989

"Political World"
"Where Teardrops Fall"
"Everything is Broken"
"Ring Them Bells"
"Man in the Long Black Coat"
"Most of the Time"
"What Good Am I?"
"Disease of Conceit"
"What Was It You Wanted"
"Shooting Star"

Under the Red Sky

When *Under the Red Sky* materialized in the fall of 1990,
I greeted it with annoyance. After the fathomless
revelations of *Oh Mercy*, it instantly felt slight, and it
sounded hideous. Its opening track, "Wiggle Wiggle," an inane
stab at infantile eroticism, took me out of the game at once. It
seemed like Dylan was back to his slovenly old ways, and I dismissed the record with the wave of a hand.

Separated and still living in my broke-down palace, I had
other things on my mind at that juncture, like a mid-life crisis.
That March, I had met a blonde, shapely photographer from
San Francisco at the South By Southwest Music Conference, and
after three entertainingly depraved days in Austin, I started fly-
ing up to the Bay Area to see her. After she unceremoniously
dumped me in favor of an itinerant musician, I moved on to
a campaign with a publicist who handled hardcore gangsta rap
acts. All I wanted to do was drink and fuck, and I stuck to that
program rigorously. Probing the finer points of an at best sec-
ond-rate Bob Dylan album was not at the top of the checklist.

Thus it would be some time, decades actually, before I returned to this problematic entry in Dylan's catalog, and when I
did I realized that it was not entirely as bad as I had first believed,
which is not to say I thought it was very good.

Producing Bob Dylan was a task that had defeated other
men, and no victory was in store for David and Don Was, the
maestros of the bizarre rock-funk act Was (Not Was). Their
strengths lay in lashing Detroit-style funk, jazz, and rock into
their loopy sound, but none of their characteristic approach was
in evidence. At times it sounded as if they were laboring mightily to make a Bob Dylan Album, as on "Handy Dandy," a silly and banal "Like a Rolling Stone" instrumental rip that came

complete with self-parodying Al Kooper organ accompaniment. At others, songs were placed in settings whose obviousness only emphasized their threadbare, jury-rigged construction: Witness the tepid Howlin' Wolf pastiche that is "10,000 Men," or the refried boogie of "Unbelievable." Heavy artillery was rolled into the fray – George Harrison, David Crosby, Elton John, Stevie Ray and Jimmie Vaughan, David Lindley, Bruce Hornsby, and (?!) Slash – but nothing jelled behind Dylan's frequently enfeebled vocals.

For his part, Dylan sounded disinterested, and it often appeared that he could barely muster the energy to push a vocal out of his throat. Much of the material was little better than doggerel – the afore-mentioned "Wiggle Wiggle," "Handy Dandy," and "Cat's in the Wall." They were like something you'd hear in kindergarten; the title song, on the other hand, was an incomprehensible fairy tale, a Brothers Grimm outtake. When Dylan took a stab at humor, you can fairly hear his joints creaking: "T.V. Talkin' Song" was a jape reminiscent of his talking blues or his comedic "Dreams" of the early days, with the weakest punch line imaginable.

Still, a few of the tunes revealed a modicum of weight. While it is finally scuttled by an enervated and uncertain Dylan vocal, "Born In Time" is nonetheless a beauty of a composition, a number that would not have been out of place on *Oh Mercy* (for which it was written, I would learn). And, though they both inexplicably fade out during Dylan's vocals, "2 X 2" and "God Knows" bear some of the heft of prophecy. Reading that Bible had been good for something.

The assets seem in the end accidental. With no one to light a real fire under him as Daniel Lanois had, Dylan had returned to the first-take work ethic of his '80s recordings. There was satisfactory stuff on *Under the Red Sky*, but "satisfactory" didn't cut it after Dylan had proven he could again be brilliant.

Released September 11, 1990

"Wiggle Wiggle"
"Under the Red Sky"
"Unbelievable"
"Born in Time"
"TV Talkin' Song"
"10,000 Men"
"2 x 2"
"God Knows"
"Handy Dandy"
"Cat's in the Well"

Good As I Been to You

Dylan needed to regroup, and he did so in his home studio with his acoustic guitar. And thus in 1992 he released his first album containing not a single song he wrote himself. Instead he presented himself to us again as he was first manifested, as a folk singer interpreting mostly traditional material.

After the initial shock of this unexpected retrenchment wore off, we could settle into the songs themselves. There were well-traveled ballads both familiar ("Blackjack Davey") and comparatively obscure ("Arthur McBride", "Jim Jones"), of both American and British origin. Blues was the bedrock here, with interpretations of songs by the Mississippi Sheiks, Blind Boy Fuller, and some models from Dylan's Village days — Rev. Gary Davis, Mississippi John Hurt, and Lonnie Johnson. Mountain music was represented by a cornerstone of the Stanley Brothers' repertoire, "Little Maggie." Acknowledging a great songwriter of the preceding century, he drafted Stephen Foster's "Hard Times." And the record closed with a pair of songs that explicitly nodded at his folk progenitors: "Diamond Joe" was drawn from Ramblin' Jack Elliott's songbook, while the epic "Froggie Went A Courtin'" paid homage to Woody Guthrie's and Pete Seeger's recordings for children.

Here was the fabric of folk music, with its colorful original cast – the murderesses, convicts, demon lovers, damsels in disguise, pistol-packin' mamas, pugnacious anti-militarists, cowboys, and rounders of all varieties who animated the songs that Dylan had used as the scaffolding for his own Sistine renderings. They had moved through his own songs like ghosts; here he conjured them whole, as they were a-borning. No one, not even Dylan, had made a record quite like this one in a while. It was a prescient move, for within five years Harry Smith's *Anthology of American Folk Music* thrust itself back into the collective consciousness.

It was a pleasure to hear Dylan cleansing his artistic palate in this unadorned format, picking with vigor and interpreting the antique tunes in his cask-aged voice with sensitivity and understanding. Nothing seems perfunctory. There's a concentration and warmth on *Good As I Been to You* lacking in many of the performances of Dylan's own material. The album's loveliness only revealed itself more deeply on repeated listenings; the more you paid attention to the narratives, the more enveloped you became.

Though I didn't listen to it a great deal upon its arrival, it proved a tonic nonetheless. I'd met the woman who would become my second wife, and life seemed good and rich again. This balanced work of darkness and light and ancient, comforting echoes suited my mood when I drew it out.

Released November 3, 1992

"Frankie & Albert"
"Jim Jones"
"Black Jack Davey"
"Canadee-i-o"
"Sittin' On Top of the World"
"Little Maggie"
"Hard Times"
"Step It Up and Go"
"Tomorrow Night"
"Arthur McBride"
"You're Gonna Quit Me"
"Diamond Joe"
"Froggie Went a-Courtin'"

World Gone Wrong

D ylan repeats himself; not an especially encouraging development. In 1993, he returned to his home studio and cut another album's worth of folk and roots material. Though it garnered more praise than its predecessor *Good As I Been to You, World Gone Wrong* seems a lesser effort in almost every aspect. It was certainly hard to complain about the material, drawn from the books of the old originators (the Mississippi Sheiks again, Blind Willie McTell, the astonishing Frank Hutchison) and Dylan's folk contemporaries (the New Lost City Ramblers, Hazel Dickens and Alice Gerrard, Doc Watson). "Blood in My Eyes" is an exclamation point, and Bob tears into McTell's "Broke Down Engine" with both hands. But overall the performances feel less engaged, and the recording is distant and messy in ways the earlier one never was. Most of the traditional tropes had been explored with more passion and precision already. Maybe this won a Grammy because "Froggy Went A Courtin'" wasn't on it.

You could hear the meter running on this one. I reviewed it with kindness for *Billboard* and filed it away. I got married for the second time that summer, and my friends Phil and Dave Alvin played at the reception, so I guess you could say this music was never far away, even if it was not always being played by Bob Dylan.

Released October 26, 1993

"World Gone Wrong"
"Love Henry"
"Ragged & Dirty"
"Blood in My Eyes"

"Broke Down Engine"
"Delia"
"Stack A Lee"
"Two Soldiers"
"Jack-A-Roe"
"Lone Pilgrim"

MTV Unplugged

I never saw the 1994 MTV telecast from which this album is drawn – I wasn't watching much TV at that point, and Bob Dylan hadn't released a new original song in four years — so all I can talk about is the recorded artifact. Dylan runs down a diverse sampling of his repertoire before a noisily demonstrative audience. The set is not in fact "unplugged," for although Dylan had wanted to perform acoustic folk material for the show, he was vetoed by the network, and instead essayed his songs in front of his touring band of the era. It was a strong one, with guitarist Bucky Baxter breathing life into the warhorses and the obscurities alike.

Some of the familiar crowd-pleasers from the First Electric Era were to be anticipated, and they are performed well, if without great distinction, and Dylan's vocal mannerisms jar only occasionally. A few surprises come in the choice of material. The season of rebirth with Daniel Lanois is represented by "Shooting Star" and a previously unheard song, "Dignity," which had been released in remixed form on a greatest hits package two days before the MTV taping. While I've never found the latter song especially appealing, its presence shows that Dylan had not given up the ghost on exploring his latter-day original music.

"Desolation Row" is a risky choice, given its length and attenuated construction, and Dylan and his band give it a slithering treatment. The two most striking and unexpected numbers are drawn from the folk-icon epoch. "With God On Our Side" may be more effective in its countrified presentation here than it was in the brooding original version on *The Times They Are A-Changin'*. (The title song from that collection, also cut for MTV, is flatter. I found that Dylan's old anthems did not play well in their middle age.)

The jaw-dropper is "John Brown," a scathing anti-war song that Dylan had never released on one of his own albums, but instead issued, under the pseudonym "Blind Boy Grunt," on a 1963 album produced by *Broadside*, the New York folk music magazine. The Gulf War was only three years behind us in '94, and it must have been on Dylan's mind as he sang of the maimed soldier dropping his worthless medals into his flag-waving mother's hand. After three decades, it had not lost its puissance.

In all, it was a respectable and sometimes even surprising turn. But it was also another live album, another stop-gap. I had to wonder at the time if *Oh Mercy* had been an anomaly, a lightning bolt in the gathering creative darkness.

Released April 25, 1995

"Tombstone Blues"
"Shooting Star"
"All Along the Watchtower"
"The Times They Are a-Changin'"
"John Brown"
"Rainy Day Women #12 & 35"
"Desolation Row"
"Dignity"
"Knockin' On Heaven's Door"
"Like a Rolling Stone"
"With God On Our Side"

Time Out of Mind

He almost died after making this. The malady had a touch of the poetic to it: an inflammation around the heart. So, when *Time Out of Mind* arrived, four months after Dylan had been hospitalized, it bore an element of the precognitive. Sometimes the hand of Death will lightly touch your collar, and you feel it and the hackles rise. Clearly Bob had sensed that someone was in the room with him. It was exactly for that reason that I'd quit drinking three years before. That cold old man with the scythe had laid his palm on my neck at 50,000 feet, on a drunken, pilled-up flight back from Florida, and I didn't want him to shake me hard by the shoulders.

There was no reason to expect that Dylan's brush with the Reaper would be immediately succeeded by something extraordinary. He'd been largely malingering for a decade, and it had been eight years since he'd pulled together an album of original songs that could be called wholly distinguished. *Time Out of Mind* surprised many who had been paying attention, and stunned most who hadn't.

Steeped in mortality and broken love, it was a record that was almost wholly congruent in sound and feel, even though its large cast of players – Dylan's working band, augmented by such hot hands as Jim Dickinson, Augie Meyers, Duke Robillard, and Cindy Cashdollar – shifted from track to track. It worked because it was constructed as a mood piece by co-conspirator Daniel Lanois, who had previously worked his studio juju on *Oh Mercy*.

Again the songs hovered thickly in the air above the listener's head, humid with loss and dread. They sprawled, as the album did – its running time was just one minute shy of *Blonde On Blonde's* 74 minutes, and all but two of the tracks were elongated over the five-minute mark. It was as if Dylan constantly kept finding something new to say, and the verses spread outward and outward, a constant ripple of ideas, each verse building upon the last.

In keeping with his themes, he sang them in a voice that was hoarse and decayed. He was not yet truly old – only 56 when the album was released – but every note creaked with age, with the effort of continuing to live life. Later we would learn that Dylan had asked Lanois to listen to Charley Patton's recordings of the '20s before the recording sessions began. The bluesman was no more than 43 when he died in 1934, yet his singing also bespoke the effort of making it one more mile down that dirt road. He was a fitting vocal avatar, and Dylan was an adept pupil.

You had to look back to *Slow Train Coming* to find a group of compositions that were as unified in tone and as impelled in performance. Then Dylan felt he was close to God; here he was on top of himself. On the majority of the numbers, Dylan looked back on his relationships – or maybe just one relationship (is that you, Sara? Carolyn?), for there's no way of telling – with weariness, regret, longing, fatigue. "Love Sick," "Standing in the Doorway," "Million Miles," "'Til I Fell in Love With You," "Cold Irons Bound," "Can't Wait" – more blood was being spilled on the tracks. Even the bouncing blues of "Dirt Road Blues" offers little hope for salvation. (It's somehow appropriate that the album's weakest song, "Make You Feel My Love," is a straight-up love song, one soggy enough to be instantly covered by Billy Joel and Garth Brooks.) And just up ahead, in "Tryin' to Get to Heaven" and "Not Dark Yet," you could see virtually nothing but bleak signposts: bridge out, not a through street, no exit, dead end.

But if *Time Out of Mind* was filled with Chaos and Old Night, its final track presented something like a dawning. "Highlands" is a song that doesn't play well in a living room; its 16-minutes-plus length is taxing if you're inert, and its loping, endlessly recycling structure can lull you right out of the plot, such as it is. I learned that it played best if you were listening to it during a long walk, because Bob is out for a stroll in the song, too. He's restless, dissatisfied, bored, lonely; his mind is flitting around, and he's itching for something he can't put his finger on. He can't just sit at home, because the neighbors tell him to turn down the Neil Young album he's playing (*Zuma? Ragged Glory?*). Shopping doesn't look like it'll get the job done, either, though a full-length leather coat might be nice. He stops into a diner for a break, and gets into a flirtatious tiff with a pretty, caustic waitress who doesn't admire his drawing skills and implies he's a sexist. Did Robert Burns have days like this one?

Rambling around town with Dylan can be some funny shit, in spite of the darkness of his mood. It's a new style for him — declarative, dialog-based, and it gives him to us at the most *human* level, bemused, pissed-off, distracted, alert to the annoying and the engaging elements of humdrum existence. It lifts the weight off the rest of the album; in the end you can see some sun shining on his back door. Even if it isn't quite bright enough for him, "that's good enough for now."

What an elegant and accomplished thing this record is. The artistic dimensions of the man are audible in virtually every second of it.

Late that year, I went to see Dylan at the tiny El Rey Theatre in L.A. People watched the gig with their mouths hanging open. I was upstairs in the VIP section, and I was so transfixed I wasn't aware of my surroundings. During one break between songs, I turned my head, and found that I was standing next to Joni Mitchell.

Released September 30, 1997

"Love Sick"
"Dirt Road Blues"
"Standing in the Doorway"
"Million Miles"
"Tryin' to Get to Heaven"

"'Til I Fell in Love With You"
"Not Dark Yet"
"Cold Irons Bound"
"Make You Feel My Love"
"Can't Wait"
"Highlands"

"Love and Theft"

On Sept. 11, 2001, I woke up early enough to watch United Flight 175 crash into the World Trade Center on live TV. In Playa Del Rey, where I was living at the time, an unearthly silence settled, as the planes that usually split the air with their takeoffs at the airport nearby were grounded. The towers fell during my bus ride to work. I was charged with writing *Billboard*'s lead story about the attacks, and spent the day talking to freaked-out music industry executives and severely traumatized co-workers who had weaved their way into the office through the Manhattan chaos. After 10 hours at my desk, I came home to discover my wife improvising a bed on the living room floor. She asked me for a divorce.

"Love and Theft" was released that day.

I soon found myself listening to Dylan's album through two small, cheap speakers hooked up to a DiscMan in my friend Dave's Sherman Oaks guesthouse. I was living out of a single canvas bag, which ironically enough my wife had given to me as a Christmas present. I had taken just a handful of albums with me – a new box of Charley Patton's blues recordings, Billie Holiday's early Columbia sides, *A Love Supreme, Astral Weeks*. Misery and transcendence were the musical order of the day. It's probably a good thing that I hadn't reached for *Time Out of Mind*, for I might have killed myself.

Love and Theft said the right things to me. Unlike its predecessor, the new album was upbeat, thank God. Where the previous record had whispered and echoed, groaning with demolished love and looming death, this one bopped and swaggered and, at times, crooned. On certain tracks it sounded as if Bing Crosby had become Dylan's unlikely latter-day role model. There were blues and old-school rockers, which could have been readily anticipated, but also songs that moved with a lilting swing. Dylan had produced it himself, and his working band – a stellar one, with Larry Campbell and Charlie Sexton leading the way — provided the accompaniment for his crabbed, thrashed voice. The sound had presence, and beauty.

It was an album that wore its derivations like medals, to be sure, but the familiarity at the music's core was reassuring. I had no quarrel with Dylan's appropriation of old Tin Pan Alley stylings on "Bye & Bye" and "Moonlight," even though this was the music he himself had purportedly rendered obsolete in the 1960s. The cheer of those tunes was winning, but not simply nostalgic; the sweetness of '20s and '30s pop was drained from them, and the lyrics bore a personal stamp. Certainly Dylan's homage to Patton in "High Water" dovetailed with my other obsessive listening at that moment; I had been swept away in a flood of my own. The churning, slamming "Lonesome Day Blues," "Honest With Me," and "Cry a While" (yes, definitely "Cry a While") lifted my unsettled mood.

To be sure, time and love had branded me with their claws, too, but Dylan had completely rediscovered his sense of humor, and that was a blessing that could not be overvalued in my book at that hour. I had to laugh at the audacity and assurance with which he crammed words into the soft shoe of "Po' Boy." He had become that "song and dance man" he had joked about in 1966. It was a companionable record, warm and funny even when dealing with the hardest truths of life, and I was buoyed by it at a time when I had no idea how or where I was going to land.

And then of course there was "Mississippi." I vaguely remembered Sheryl Crow's version of the song, which had glanced off my ear and moved on. Dylan's own rendition, chiming yet weighty with regret and hinting at the apocalyptic, struck me as a work of balanced perfection. I never responded to the song simply on an aesthetic level. Its rising melody, rhythmic certainty, and its graceful gaze into the uncertainty of love, and the sound of Dylan's voice, weary yet somehow hopeful, drew me up to my feet in a moment when I was not sure I could raise myself off my knees. I listened to it over and over, and when I play it today I am seldom able to play it just once.

I feel the same way about "Things Have Changed."

Released September 11, 2001

"Tweedle Dee & Tweedle Dum"
"Mississippi"
"Summer Days"
"Bye and Bye"
"Lonesome Day Blues"
"Floater (Too Much to Ask)"
"High Water (For Charley Patton)"
"Moonlight"
"Honest With Me"
"Po' Boy"
"Cry a While"
"Sugar Baby"

Modern Times

I t had been five years since his last album, and newly-engraved trophies had lined his mantelpiece in the interim, so I eagerly attended a private playback of *Modern Times* at the Santa Monica office of Bob Dylan's publicist in 2006. I left impressed, perhaps overly so. The record's assets could be apprehended immediately, and it appeared Dylan had remained in the groove he had cut with his previous two works. However, the more I listened, the more he seemed to be stuck in it.

Some of my ultimate disappointment stemmed from the band, which included my friend Denny Freeman, one of Austin's most estimable and versatile guitarists, and a cat I dearly love. I'd seen the group the previous year at a concert (opened by a show-stealing Merle Haggard) at Hollywood's Pantages Theatre. They looked terrified. Perhaps some of that fear persisted, for while the group supplied a seamless backdrop for Dylan's desiccated singing with great clarity, they appeared unwilling to ever put the pedal to the floor, whereas the previous Sexton-Campbell unit could lullaby you into a slumber or kick in your teeth in equal measure. The enterprise had a muffled quality to it. Possibly the musicians worried about overpowering the now 65-year-old Dylan's vocals, which were growing increasingly enfeebled as his years of compulsive touring wore on.

The biggest problem was the songs, which in the main lacked any staying power in the stretch. Several of them were blues readymades: Hambone Willie Newburn's "Rollin' and Tumblin'" and Memphis Minnie and Kansas Joe's "When the Levee Breaks" (retooled as "The Levee's Gonna Break") were the subjects of fairly straightforward lifts, while "Someday Baby" owed its life to Muddy Waters' "Trouble No More." The ballads, too, tipped their hat to melodies of the nearly prehistoric Gene Austin era.

Modern Times: quite the misnomer. Too often, the lyrics used old blues lines as placeholders, and many of the collection's attenuated numbers – only one of which ran under five minutes, and that one not by much – sported texts that felt unsifted, in a first-thought-best-thought manner. And…Alicia Keys? *Please.*

There were still things to marvel at. "When the Deal Goes Down," with its titular nod to Robert Johnson and Charlie Poole, was a delicately affecting waltz with lyrics that cohered in a way they seldom did elsewhere on the record. And the album closer, the hushed and somewhat menacing "Ain't Talkin'," though it too seemed scrambled and lyrically hyperactive, held enough uneasiness and horror to grab the listener.

Modern Times did play well, and it satisfied enough people to become Dylan's first No. 1 album in 30 years. But though it was considered by many (but not by the man who made it) as the conclusion of a trilogy of albums, it plainly differed from its two predecessors, both of which had exerted a firm grip on me emotionally. Remote and even a little studied, it was a twice-told tale, and it required *effort* to listen to it repeatedly. I had never found that to be a quality of a first-rate Bob Dylan record.

Released August 29, 2006

"Thunder on the Mountain"
"Spirit on the Water"
"Rollin' and Tumblin'"
"When the Deal Goes Down"
"Someday Baby"
"Workingman's Blues #2"
"Beyond the Horizon"
"Nettie Moore"
"The Levee's Gonna Break"
"Ain't Talkin'"

Together Through Life

Exhaustion and ongoing benign thievery characterized the music on *Together Through Life*, which had its roots in a commissioned soundtrack for a film by French director Olivier Dahan that never received a U.S. theatrical release. (Renee Zellweger can be heard performing "Life is Hard" in its trailer.) Dylan apparently couldn't be troubled to pull together the music on his own, so he turned to erstwhile Grateful Dead lyricist Robert Hunter, with whom he partnered for two songs on the execrable *Down in the Groove*, to co-write most of the songs.

The poaching had gotten so extreme that Willie Dixon, dead for 17 years, was credited as co-author of "My Wife's Home Town," whose key lick and arrangement were pilfered wholesale from the late blues songwriter's Muddy Waters hit "Just Make Love to Me" (aka "I Just Want to Make Love to You"). "Beyond Here Lies Nothing" went the "Black Magic Woman" route and stole the superstructure of Otis Rush's "All Your Love (I Missing Loving)." "It's All Good" was a cranked-up clone of Billy Boy Arnold's "Got Love If You Want It." "If You Ever Go to Houston" was launched off a line from Leadbelly's "Midnight Special." Dylan's pen had run completely dry.

He was now firmly installed as his own pseudonymous producer, so there was no one in the booth to hit the talk-back button and say, "Uh, Bob, maybe we should try another take." His blown-out voice was unable to animate any of the up-tempo material, so it's a blessing that a pair of ballads, "Forgetful Heart" and "This Dream of You," served as the album's strongest material. The latter, the lone solo composition on the record, a border-flavored love song graced by David Hidalgo's accordion and sweet uncredited fiddle work (probably by Donnie Herron of Dylan's working band), did not strain Dylan's vocal capabilities, and the frailty of his singing lent a moving quality to the work, which was far superior to anything else on the disc.

Overall, it was Dylan's weakest entry in a decade, well played enough to set it apart from the full-blown catastrophes of years past, but without any real distinction or much certifiable brilliance. But his evidently bulletproof late-career rep nonetheless pushed *Together Through Life* to the top of the American chart.

I was nonplussed by the degradation of Dylan's output. At that moment he appeared to be far from his muse. Out of loyalty, I played a couple of tracks on my online radio show, knowing full well that the current vintage was far from top-shelf stuff.

Released April 27, 2009

"Beyond Here Lies Nothing"
"Life is Hard"
"My Wife's Home Town"
"If You Ever Go to Houston"
"Forgetful Heart"
"Jolene"
"This Dream of You"
"Shake Shake Mama"
"I Feel a Change Comin' On"
"It's All Good"

Christmas in the Heart

Conceptually, *Christmas in the Heart* will endure as one of the perfect works of the 21st century: Bob Dylan sings hymns, carols, and Yuletide pop tunes in his worn-out catarrh, like your ancient drunken uncle at the dinner table, well into his second bottle of peppermint schnapps. The mere fact that such a daffy thing exists delights me.

I began playing something off in December every year as part of the seasonal programming on my radio show. You may find other uses for it, like clearing the house of unwelcome guests as the holiday party winds down.

Tidings of comfort and joy? Maybe not comfort, but joy, in some quantity, to be sure. I scratched my head when this album was released, as a benefit project, in 2009, but now it makes me laugh, often out loud, and some of it is even legitimately heart-warming. Sure, it's mainly high camp, regardless of stated or even actual intent. Put it on the stereo, and irony trickles out of the speakers. It's an arch new-millennium shot at making the kind of Christmas music, alternately jovial and devout, that Dylan grew up listening to during the '40s and '50s. The damn thing kicks off with sleigh bells! I wish he'd billed the cooing backup vocalists as the Bob Dylan Singers, just to complete the effect.

OK, much of this is terrible, and Dylan's voice is shot to hell. I would rather have my kneecaps broken with sledgehammers than listen to his "Have Yourself a Merry Little Christmas" ever again. But this album has its bright spots. To wit:

1) We get to hear Bob Dylan sing in Latin ("Adeste Fideles") and, briefly, in Hawaiian ("Christmas Island").
2) The polka kicks ass.
3) Bob's version of "The Christmas Blues" is far bluesier than Dean Martin's.

4) I love the way he rasps "Amen" at the end of "O Little
   Town of Bethlehem." And the way he says "Ho, ho, ho" on
   "Must Be Santa," as only Bob Dylan can say "Ho, ho, ho."

Merry Christmas to all, and to all a goodnight.

Released October 17, 2009

"Here Comes Santa Claus"
"Do You Hear What I Hear?"
"Winter Wonderland"
"Hark the Herald Angels Sing"
"I'll Be Home For Christmas"
"Little Drummer Boy"
"O' Come All Ye Faithful (Adeste Fidelis)"
"Have Yourself a Merry Little Christmas"
"Must Be Santa"
"Silver Bells"
"The First Noel"
"Christmas Island"
"The Christmas Song"
"O' Little Town of Bethlehem"

Tempest

So here we are in the present, or as close as we will get to it. But does time really exist for Bob Dylan?

The greatness of *Tempest* revealed itself to me slowly, like a train rising over the distant horizon, puffing out of the past, like the one in "Duquesne Whistle." I love the way this tune, co-written with Robert Hunter, kicks off, faintly, like an old 78, except without any corny surface noise effects. We're criss-crossing the country, counting the cross ties on the line, hearing the miles click by, traveling into America's dark earth, running our fingers over the dimensions of the land.

The voice is scorched, but the eye is keen, the heart uncertain but beating loud. The album, the rest of it comprising new Dylan originals, reflects its title in a storm of invention. Dylan knows what it feels like to be alone at midnight, to quiver in rage against one's enemies and thirst for their blood, to trail down to Scarlet Town where Desolation Row's streets are still teeming. But he can still rock down that narrow way, and dance like Bo Diddley (oh, yeah) before the thrones of the early Roman kings.

I imagine Bob in his study, old portraits on the wall, listening closely to *People Take Warning!* That 2007 compilation contained no less than seven tracks devoted to the sinking of the *RMS Titanic*, already 100 years behind us. Determined to outdo them all with his own centennial statement, he plunged into the tale for 14 minutes, directing a cast stretching from ill-fated Captain Smith to Leonardo DiCaprio. Mission accomplished. Maybe the same set's disc of murder ballads thrust him back to the Child song catalog, where one finds "Young Hunting," known in another form as "Henry Lee," whose title character initiates the carnage in Dylan's "Tin Angel." Again, he's trying to top all comers, and wading through a tangle of infidelity and a river of Grand Guignol gore he claims the prize again.

This is a work so masterful it should come bound in leather covers. The songs are vast, but there is never the sense that they are saying either not enough or too much; each is complete on its own assured terms. The band – the road group, with returnee Charlie Sexton and MVP sideman David Hidalgo – is the soul of economy and sympathy. The music, while still roots-based, was more expansive; there wasn't any recent precedent for the cascading "Long and Wasted Years," for instance. Vocally, Dylan wears the mantle of age with rough grace and cunning. His limitations become assets here.

Tempest concludes with an elegy to John Lennon, 32 years in the making. Scraps of Beatles lyrics lean poignantly against a William Blake illumination and a child's prayer. Dylan isn't afraid to be mawkish at times in his homage to another shape-shifting artist who rode the '60s whirlwind. He has nothing to be ashamed of, for the emotion rings true. Listening to this song, I was again hurled back in time, recalling a fugitive film clip from 1966, Dylan and Lennon in the back of a London limo, Dylan dead drunk and green at the gills, Lennon grinning with his keen blade drawn, hidden behind their shades. *("I wear dark glasses to cover my eyes/There are secrets in 'em I can't disguise.")* And I remembered that it was a little more than a month after I received my first Bob Dylan album that "I Want to Hold Your Hand" hit my transistor radio, like a gale.

Contrary to Dylan's disclaimer of any titular allusion, this record is Shakespearean.

I listened to the album again sitting on a bench in the park near my home, watching the methane bubble up from the La Brea Tar Pits, where all time is visible, as it is in the best of Bob Dylan's music. It was near the closing of the year, and the park was full of vacationing people – tourists dropping by museums, families on their outings, solitary citizens like myself rambling in the sunshine. Nearby the resident street musician, fitted out in his cowboy hat and vest, played his banjo, bawling out traditional folk tunes that could be found in the repertoire of another, better-known performer.

Under brilliant December light I watched the world roll by, and wondered if the people in the park knew that they were all in a Bob Dylan song. They are, you know, for his music contains everything.

Released September 10, 2012

"Duquesne Whistle"
"Soon After Midnight"
"Narrow Way"
"Long and Wasted Years"
"Pay in Blood"
"Scarlet Town"
"Early Roman Kings"
"Tin Angel"
""

"Roll On John"

Shadows in the Night

Her hair was still red.

I hadn't seen her for 20 years. Back then, she was fresh out of college. I was newly married. We were not close, colleagues only, but one night in 1994 she had sat with me in a dimly lit hotel room in Florida as I went down my hellhole. I did not touch her, though I may very much have wanted to.

Now, at a homecoming of sorts in a crowded barroom, she brushed my lips with small drunken kisses, three or four, I can't recall exactly how many, and then (she would not remember this later) she slid onto my lap, holding my hand tightly.

And I was gone, off to the races.

She had two young children and lived in a house in a far-flung suburb. She was trying to restart her writing career. Her marriage of a dozen years was crashing, and the tumult of impending divorce was rising as swiftly as her husband's untethered wrath. In the first bloom of middle age, she was beautiful and quite brilliant, and she emanated the same subtle heat she did when she was young. She also possessed an exquisite recklessness, though most would not think so to look at her; I'd known it from the first, long ago, and it impelled my desire, which was fierce and immediate.

We soon rendezvoused again, twice, chastely. She went to New York for the holidays, to pursue work and, I knew, other things. I had sworn that I would not press her during her escape, but after days of silence, on Christmas I sent her a long letter, yes, one of those, a characteristic, passionate blunder. I heard nothing from her until after the New Year; she called during the long car ride from LAX to her home. Her plate was too full, and there was no room on it for me. Yet in the days that followed she would reach out to me – sometimes with long phone calls that consumed the hours after midnight, sometimes in glancing messages on social media that I decoded with ease. We would talk of writing, her marriage, her roiling life; once, at 2 a.m., she told me she felt empty. My snapped heart, so full of her, would keep me awake until a gray dawn seeped through my shades.

She played constantly in the back of my mind, but I had a book to finish. I returned to *Blood On the Tracks* and *Oh Mercy*, those reliable life preservers, and to songs, sad old ones, like "Girl From the North Country" and "Boots of Spanish Leather." I found new beauty in an album I had once found slightly chilly, *Time Out of Mind*, and its sorrowful love songs – "Love Sick," "Standing in the Doorway," "Million Miles," "'Til I Fell in Love With You" – played fresh as newly spilled blood. But my last chapter landed, in perfect form, in January, when *Shadows in the Night* reached me.

Word of the album had surfaced the previous spring: It would be a collection of standards, most of them ballads, from the Great American Songbook, all of them previously interpreted, some of them multiple times, by Frank Sinatra. Many professed to be nonplussed. The disconnect – beyond the incongruity of Dylan paying homage to a singer's singer – took the form of a simple question: What had Dylan to do with Sinatra's music, anyway? He was after all removing himself far from his métier – folk, blues, country, rock, the American roots.

For me, the answer was simple: Dylan had *grown up* with that music, as I had grown up with Dylan's. I naturally felt a complete kinship with his enterprise. Dylan was less than a year old when Sinatra began his solo career in 1942. He likely heard some of Sinatra's wartime and postwar hits – "Night and Day," "Oh What It Seemed to Be," "Day By Day," "September Song" – as a child, possibly on the radios his father sold in his Hibbing appliance store. Maybe as a toddler his parents had dragged him to see *Anchors Aweigh*, Sinatra's first big movie vehicle, or tuned in to his weekly radio show. As a teenager, he was almost certainly exposed to the resurgent star's great, anguished Capitol concept albums of the '50s – In *the Wee Small Hours, Only the Lonely, Where Are You?, No One Cares*; those LPs were omnipresent, inescapable. *The Blood On the Tracks* of their day, if you will.

Dylan was a child of those Tin Pan Alley songs, those durable statements of longing, lust, and suffering, as much as he may have publicly mocked and scorned their origins in the past. Their craft, their beauty, and their emotion sang to him. He believed in them thoroughly.

It's possibly forgotten by some that though they reigned on different sides of a generational and cultural gulf, Sinatra and Dylan occupied the same space at exactly the same time for a while: the record charts. In 1966, weeks before the release of *Blonde On Blonde*, the 50-year-old Sinatra issued the biggest solo single of his latter-day career, the No. 1 hit "Strangers in the Night." Though seemingly nothing alike and separated in age by a quarter century, Dylan and Sinatra were peers of a sort, looming simultaneously over the same American artistic landscape, posing dramatically different profiles, musing on the same perils and pitfalls of romance from radically different perspectives. It was left to Dylan to show how entwined they were at the core.

Dylan had offered explicit homage to the elder statesman in 1995, when he appeared on an all-star TV special on the eve of Sinatra's 80th birthday. Backed by his working band and a string section, Dylan played "Restless Farewell," the suitably intransigent number heard on *The Times They Are A-Changin'*. In a shot taken from the stage, Sinatra, a man of that song as much as its author was, is seen watching the performance, hand under his chin, intent, inscrutable.

It may well be that Dylan recalled that performance when he was preparing to make what became *Shadows in the Night*. The TV appearance was dominated by the keening steel guitar work of Bucky Baxter. Two decades later, Dylan's current guitarist Donnie Herron floated immense, hovering clouds of steel over a recital of 10 standards, most of them about battered hearts and loss.

In my hobbled, uncertain state, I felt I had lost already, and if ever there was a record I was emotionally prepared to hear in the instant, this was it.

The first track drawn from the album, "Full Moon and Empty Arms," appeared online in April of 2014, when the set was scheduled for imminent release. (Pushed back, it arrived, appropriately enough, in February of 2015, Sinatra's centennial year.) Herron's steel, complemented by brush strokes from fellow guitarists Charlie Sexton and Stu Kimball, cloaked the song in a shower of country teardrops, while Tony Garnier – whose tenure with Dylan stretches back to the Sinatra special — plucked a standup bass. Drummer George Receli goes virtually unheard, here and elsewhere; save for some lightly brushed snare, a cymbal tap or two, and an album-closing tympani roll, he lays out for the proceedings. His absence creates a dreamy hush, a literally timeless one. Dylan's vocals came as something of a surprise. While his throat was still seared and his intonation uncertain, and he missed the bull's eye on several notes, his approach to the song was unmannered, respectful, and soulful. He was singing with care, of a sort unheard in his work since the '90s at least.

That first offering came bearing an interesting subtext. "Full Moon and Empty Arms" was a top-20 hit for Sinatra in 1945; the same year, David Lean's film *Brief Encounter* reached theaters. The song is based on Sergei Rachmaninoff's Piano Concerto No. 2, which — as Dylan was no doubt aware — serves as an incessant underscore through most of Lean's eviscerating drama about an affair in pre-war England between a doctor and a housewife, both married. Pain crowds every frame of the picture, one of the most tortured screen love stories of them all, and it similarly suffuses nearly every track on *Shadows in the Night*.

Aesthetically and perhaps personally – for, it was reported, he had just separated from his third wife — Dylan was ideally situated to feel these songs, and feel them he does, profoundly. They are especially naked performances. Dylan is close-mic'ed, and every vocal tic, tentative note, and expiring line is captured in three dimensions; on "Full Moon and Empty Arms" and "What'll I Do," he can be heard wetting his lips, or inhaling and exhaling quietly. He is in the room with you.

There is no point in bothering to make technical comparisons between Sinatra and Dylan. Yet, despite his grainy, hard-worn voice, Dylan actually does resemble Sinatra here in a couple of important ways – he is always *present*, in the moment of the song, his command of rhythm is acute, and he respects the melody and the sense of the material, which was the hallmark of Sinatra's approach throughout his long career.

Several other performances nailed me where I live. "I'm a Fool to Want You," which Sinatra co-wrote and debuted, in 1951 during his ardent pursuit of Ava Gardner, is the lead-off track on the album and, at nearly five minutes, its longest number. The song also serves as the opening track of *Lady in Satin*, the 1958 collection by Billie Holiday (who was, like Dylan, signed to Columbia Records by A&R man and producer John Hammond). Those two interpretations could not be more different in the way they're framed: Dylan's is simple and pared-down (the presence of two horns notwithstanding), while Holiday's, cut 18 months before her death, gets a lush treatment from Ray Ellis' big orchestra. Yet there are deep affinities between the performances and the albums from which they are drawn. They are wintry, scourged affairs, made by singers with impaired instruments who have retained the merest remnants of what can be called "vocal technique." The records may lack the clarity and polished skill of Sinatra's high-concept creations, yet they cut to the quick of the matter and carve you up, for the lyrics have been completely lived.

Other, more economical tracks cast their shadows. "Autumn Leaves," which wafts in on an extended, plangent introduction by Herron and the band, gets a direct, economical reading by Dylan, who gives such precise weight to each syllable that you can almost feel those blissful summer kisses, or the dry, hot texture of his lover's sunburned hand. His take on "Where Are

You?," the title song on Sinatra's melancholy 1957 album, makes the lyric's dazed yearning palpable.

A mood of gathering darkness is generally sustained until the last track. The album's only real failure comes in a song that cuts against the prevailing moonlit vibe. Rodgers and Hammerstein's "Some Enchanted Evening," the record's lone optimistic composition (and only show tune), was undoubtedly selected to lighten the texture of the work, but its blissful theme of new love abloom is unmoored amid the downbeat atmosphere; its loping arrangement and Dylan's rasping, stubbornly on-the-beat delivery scuttle the interpretation.

On one track, however, Dylan actually manages to outdo the Chairman at his own game. Sinatra's 1950 reading of Cy Coleman and Joe McCarthy's "Why Try to Change Me Now?" is an unconvincing failure, for his delivery is too steely for the whimsical material; it's impossible to imagine that this self-possessed vocalist has habits even he can't explain. Dylan's understated version is warm, *human*, daubed with humor and taking delight in its own eccentricity. We can believe him when he asks, "Don't you remember I was always your clown?"

Dylan chose to conclude *Shadows in the Night* with an old companion: "That Lucky Old Sun," a song he first performed in concert in 1985 and to which he occasionally returned into the new millennium. No less supplicating than the album's "Stay With Me" (a soundtrack obscurity from the 1964 film *The Cardinal*, and the newly-minted encore for Dylan's late-2014 shows), the 1949 composition is, in the end, a prayer in which the singer begs the Lord to lift the weight of the world off his shoulders. The rhythmic mannerisms that marred Dylan's earlier live renditions of the song are absent; stretching his flayed pipes to the limit, riding the subdued rumble of his horn-augmented band, he connects with the number until his last, failing note.

It is entirely likely that many consider *Shadows in the Night* an album that they could never, ever want. Materializing when it did, it presented itself to me as an album I absolutely needed, possibly could not live without. Those old tunes, some penned generations ago, had retained their meaning, and you can hear Dylan wringing that devastating meaning from them with every wracked fiber of his then-72-year-old being. And, in doing so, he made those songs mine again.

I wore them gratefully like a second skin as sunset still came early and night fell hard upon me. In the strange heat of February, the sun emerged to blind me, and for a handful of days we were together. I found I could tell her I loved her out loud and she would not put her fingers to my lips to silence me, and she could tell me she loved me. But nothing was simple, nothing resolved. She was living in a whirlwind, and as I lingered in solitary doubt the music still played in my head.

Then, only this afternoon, my phone rang again…

Released February 3, 2015

"I'm a Fool to Want You"
"The Night We Called It a Day"
"Stay With Me"
"Autumn Leaves"
"Why Try to Change Me Now"
"Some Enchanted Evening"
"Full Moon and Empty Arms"
"Where Are You?"
"What'll I Do"
"That Lucky Old Sun"

Fallen Angels

Time, age, and mortality weighed heavily on my shoulders as 2016 dawned. Each day seemed to bring news of the passing of a musician; some of them were heroes, some simply part of the fabric of my everyday life. One morning I awoke to learn that two of my friends on Facebook – one a man I'd known for 30 years – had died. Infirmity began to dog me: A simple cold could become an epic lasting two weeks, and an old disc injury made me feel as if I had an icepick stuck in my lower back. A bitch.

And here comes Bob Dylan, on the eve of his 75th birthday, moving towards me from the far horizon as jauntily as Frank Sinatra in the opening reel of *The Tender Trap*, telling me that fairy tales can come true if I am among the very young at heart. It struck me as sound counsel.

Many would be tempted to see Dylan's 37th studio release *Fallen Angels* as a mere continuation of the previous year's *Shadows in the Night*. But in terms of tonal quality and emotional character, the two have far less in common than did his diptych of '90s solo folk recordings, *Good As I Been to You* and *World Gone Wrong* – despite the fact that, unlike those earlier records cut four years apart, the two collections of standards and old pop tunes were largely derived from one series of recording dates in 2014 (with a brief return to the studio in February of '16 to lay down one or two numbers).

Fallen Angels mainly comprises songs taken from Sinatra's repertoire, with all but one of the 12 tracks a tune that the Voice recorded between 1939 and 1979. The lone exception – and one of three songs on the album with lyrics by Johnny Mercer – was "Skylark," written by Mercer and Hoagy Carmichael in 1941 and curiously never essayed by Sinatra during his 55-year recording career. (All of the Dylan material was recorded at the Hollywood studios of Capitol Records, the label co-founded by Mercer in 1942 and Sinatra's home from 1954-1962 and in 1993-94.)

Again, Dylan is heard backed by his working band, and his vocals are no less weathered and rheumy than they were on *Shadows in the Night*. But *Fallen Angels* isn't simply a replay of the previous record's midnight contemplation of love's abyss. Though there is loss, and sometimes skepticism, Dylan is here drawn to measuring the conventions of 20th century songcraft, and to interpreting ballads of enduring love.

Some of the repertoire is as antique as Granny's antimacassar doilies. The oldest composition on the album, "Come Rain or Come Shine," was penned by Isham Jones and Gus Kahn in 1924. Four of the songs were recorded by Sinatra in the earliest days of his career; these include "Melancholy Mood," his very first single (cut with Harry James' band in 1939), and his first hit, "All or Nothing at All" (a feature with James the same year).

A few might make a contemporary listener wince. "Polka Dots and Moonbeams," which Sinatra first recorded in 1940 during his tenure with Tommy Dorsey's orchestra, first raised my hackles as a teenager when I heard it on *A Man and His Music*, the two-LP Sinatra retrospective of 1965; the singer had previously re-recorded this corny warhorse on his 1961 Dorsey homage *I Remember Tommy*. Another ancient entry, the James-era piece of oriental exotica "On a Little Street in Singapore," plays like a moonlit Marlene Dietrich love scene from an Josef von Sternberg melodrama.

Why has Dylan taken to these often overripe, backdated things? I'll turn to "Come Rain or Come Shine" in a moment, but I believe in the other cases it is because he likes the way the lyrics fall off his tongue. Dylan has always been an artist drunk with words, one who likes to crash them against each other just to hear the chime and clatter they make, and his on-point, precisely-measured, irony-free readings of the old lyrics finds him simply savoring the sound of them. There's a smile in the way he sings, "In my frightened arms, polka dots and moonbeams/sparkled on a pug-nosed dream"; dour humor in the way he grimly intones, "But love is a whimsy and as flimsy as lace/and my arms embrace an empty space"; outré image-painting as he croons, "My sails tonight are filled with perfume of Shalimar."

There's also a dandy Mercer internal rhyme – "You're the mate that fate had me created for" – in "That Old Black Magic." (Not too far from, "Once upon a time you dressed so fine, threw the bums a dime in your prime," really.) Sinatra recorded it as a string-soaked ballad for Columbia in 1946 and at a medium tempo on 1961's descriptively titled *Come Swing With Me*, but Dylan's arrangement is a straight-up copy of Louis Prima and Keely Smith's lightning jumpin'-jive duel on their hit 1958 single. Here drummer George Receli, restrained to a brushed snare when he is employed at all on the Sinatra-inspired recordings, is finally allowed to cut loose on his entire kit. Dylan's sly, rambunctious version, which comes complete with a flag-waving show-biz climax, is an exuberant and definitive break with the darkness in which *Shadows in the Night* lowered.

There are moments of sadness and doubt on *Fallen Angels* – in the glum "Melancholy Mood," the prowling "Maybe You'll Be There," and the self-doubting yet openhearted "Nevertheless." But the profound despair with which *Shadows in the Night* was bathed never invades its putative sequel for more than a passing moment. Despite its forbidding title, with its echo of original sin, the record is about a world where love is not a catastrophe, and more than a possibility – the subject of "Skylark" – but instead is deep, abiding, and eternal.

In his quintessential study "Frank Sinatra Has a Cold," published in *Esquire* 50 years ago, Gay Talese speaks of "a fierce fidelity" heard in the defining hits "All or Nothing At All" and "All the Way," both of which are interpreted on *Fallen Angels*. So too are the similarly oriented "Come Rain or Come Shine" and "It Had to Be You." These are all songs in which love is fated, committed, and forever, and Dylan understands and uncovers every intense word of them. (Stop to savor his reading of the rarely heard introductory verse in "It Had to Be You.") The subdued clouds of music that his band creates here are not the ones that cover the moon; they foreshadow a storm of passion.

Time folds back on itself in *Fallen Angels*: "Who knows where the road will lead us? Only a fool would say." *Shadows in the Night* despondently lives in the harrowing past; this album gazes hopefully into the future. As we listen to this album's most affecting performances, we are at the beginning of love, which for lovers is the beginning of time, a place where we are, if you will, forever young.

I found that I needed *Fallen Angels* as much as I had needed *Shadows in the Night*, and I will always hold these two eccentric and beautiful records, which so movingly translate these old songs into Dylan's own idiom, close in my heart.

But I found myself longing for one thing more: I wished that Dylan had attempted "This is All I Ask," the Gordon Jenkins ballad that graced Sinatra's 1965 album *September of My Years* and his TV special of the same year.

It's possible that the song's drifting melody and slowly rising climax would have eluded Dylan's vocal grasp, but I nonetheless would give anything to hear him tear into Jenkins' last lines — a perfect mirror of "Young at Heart," a sweet summation of his wintry offerings, and of what I feel in my soul, as he undoubtedly feels it in his own:

And let the music play
As long as there's a song to sing
Then I will stay younger than spring

Released May 20, 2016

"Young at Heart"
"Maybe You'll Be There"
"Polka Dots and Moonbeams"
"All the Way"
"Skylark"
"Nevertheless"
"All or Nothing at All"
"On a Little Street in Singapore"
"It Had to Be You"
"Melancholy Mood"
"That Old Black Magic"
"Come Rain or Come Shine"

Triplicate

S ometimes winter will throw everything it's got at you. In the last weeks of 2016, I took in my beloved onetime flame, newly unmoored, and her little dog, which had suddenly and frighteningly gone blind. We were an instant family in close quarters, frequently prone to the same drama that had shaken the walls of my suddenly crowded apartment in years past. She and I could sometimes be happy, though we each slept alone. Some small blessings manifested themselves: Through treatment, the dog gradually regained much of his sight. Then, just as the year turned and spring began to gently materialize after a long season of rain, I got a call out of the blue from another old lover, beset by myriad health problems in the 25 years since we parted. Now destitute and faced with eviction, her intense pain quieted by morphine and Fentanyl, she too was looking for a soft place to fall. I found what aid I could for her. She asked me to pray for her, and I did.

In these circumstances, a large serving of standard balladry from Bob Dylan, his third such work in three years, seemed a resonant gift. For, as the song says, the fundamental things apply.

Neither as somber as *Shadows in the Night* nor as relatively optimistic as *Fallen Angels*, *Triplicate* played more as a jumbo sampler of Great American Song, though its principal focus was, like its immediate predecessors, the vicissitudes of romance, and the thickets of the past. It came advertised as a thematically organized work, but its three individually titled discs promised more than they delivered; if each of the three 10-song discs contained anything like a narrative, none could be readily divined. The conceptual premise – albums-within-the-album titled *'Til the Sun Goes Down, Devil Dolls,* and *Comin' Home Late* – seemed more a fedora tip to Frank Sinatra's themed three-LP 1980 release *Trilogy: Past Present Future* than an actual artistic construct.

Once again, Sinatra's catalog was the organizing principal: Of the set's 30 numbers, only one, the ersatz Hoagy Carmichael tune "Braggin'," was not recorded by the Voice. (Dick Haymes, Sinatra's replacement in Tommy Dorsey's band, essayed this plummy, folksy swinger in 1941.) The material covers the full breadth of Sinatra's career, from his second single, recorded in 1939 as the vocalist in Harry James' band, to a number he re-recorded (as a duet with – remember him? – Jon Secada) for his final album, 1994's *Duets II*. Songs are drawn from his work with Dorsey and solo records for Columbia, Capitol, Reprise, and Qwest.

Recorded by Dylan and his poised, brilliant working band (now a quartet with the exit of Stu Kimball), augmented by guitarist Dean Parks, in a siege of sessions at Capitol Records' Hollywood facility in February 2016, *Triplicate* is a demanding work, and it is not always a rewarding one. Two years and a couple hundred live shows separated those studio dates from the 2014 stand at Capitol that produced the music on *Shadow in the Night* and *Fallen Angels*, and those busy 24 months worked like a merciless eternity on Dylan's broiled mid-septuagenarian pipes. Nowhere is the strain more visible than on the harder-swinging, horn-inflected numbers – "I Guess I'll Have to Change My Plans," "Braggin'," and "Day In, Day Out" – that misguidedly lead off the three discs.

However, beyond those tracks and a completely miscalculated rendition of the swaggering Sinatra-Basie opus "The Best is Yet to Come," Dylan's batting average is remarkably high for such a mammoth undertaking. Certainly, his voice remains as splintered as we've come to expect it, but the great majority of the performances on *Triplicate* are animated by the same sure sense of rhythm, careful delivery, and wit that made his first two standard sorties so pleasurable and revealing.

Writer Tom Piazza – who penned a liner-note encomium for the set that bears comparison to Pete Hamill's exegesis for *Blood on the Tracks* – rightly singles out Dylan's work on "How Deep is the Ocean," with its coolly erotic reading of the line, "How many times a day do I think of you?" He wrests the full affect out of Irving Berlin's classic lyric, and it's one of the record's most completely realized performances.

There are several other heart-stopping numbers here, all satisfyingly interpreted in Dylan's rough yet attuned latter-day style. "Once Upon a Time," one of three songs drawn from Sinatra's early-autumn concept set *September of My Years*, masterfully boils down Gordon Jenkins' big orchestral arrangement to a lean small-band format; Dylan is faithful to the original, right down to Sinatra's brooding single-note vocal coda "Once upon a time never comes again." "Here's That Rainy Day," "These Foolish Things" "You Go to My Head," and "Why Was I Born" exhibit a similar intense intimacy.

He draws some of the biggest guns from the classic songbook here: Three of the tunes on *Triplicate*, all of them best known in ballad performances, receive extended treatment by Sinatra scholar Will Friedwald in his 2002 study of a dozen popular masterworks, *Stardust Memories*. Harold Arlen and Ted Koehler's "Stormy Weather," owned successively by Ethel Waters, Lena Horne, and Billie Holiday, shines thanks to its wonderful setting – teeing off with a low instrumental rumble, like an approaching thunderhead, stirred by the band – and an understated Dylan reading (possibly left over from the 2014 sessions). No one is ever going to forget Dooley Wilson's reading of Herman Hupfeld's "As Time Goes By" in *Casablanca*, so Dylan decides to essentially ignore it, opting to change up the rhythm and push the tune with glimmering guitar work. All renderings of Hoagy Carmichael and Mitchell Parish's "Stardust" must of necessity line up behind Nat King Cole's profoundly deep and definitive 1957 ballad recording; once more, Dylan dodges a bullet by essaying it as a jaunty swinger, in tribute to Louis Armstrong's 1931 arrangement.

But the very greatest delights on *Triplicate* come when Dylan reaches deep into the song bag. Many of the album's most entertaining (and, frequently, most perversely funny) moments are supplied by numbers that languish in Sinatra's oeuvre as relatively unrecognized album tracks or forgotten singles. This material is raw meat for Dylan.

Take, for instance, "There's a Flaw in My Flue." Just the title of this Jimmy Van Heusen-Johnny Burke antiquity should be enough to clue in the listener that this tune, cut by Sinatra in 1953 and promptly forgotten, is sub-par material at best. But Dylan goes at it zestily, chewing at the song's labored wordplay as if it were musical filet mignon. Likewise, "When the World Was Young," Johnny Mercer's English-language adaptation of a louche, reflective French oddity, was apparently taken up just so that Dylan could proclaim himself "a boulevardier, the toast of Paree"; he makes this unpromising and mannered song moving nonetheless. He continues to draw deadpan mirth from the creakiest of phrases – "fly Lothario" in "I Guess I'll Have to Change My Plans," "an awning of silvery boughs" in "Trade Winds" – and takes audible delight in the most flyblown badinage.

What may be my favorite performance arrives exactly in the middle of *Triplicate*. You have likely cruised by "P.S. I Love You" – a 1934 Gordon Jenkins-Johnny Mercer composition not to be confused with the 1962 Beatles hit – on Sinatra's 1957 LP *Close to You*, but Dylan stops you in your tracks with it. Written in the form of an epistle from a lonely, somewhat baffled man to his absent lover, it piles up mundane detail – dishes in the sink, a cigarette-burned dining room table – with light-fingered humor. It's the sort of rueful domestic scenario that Sinatra was never able to pull off convincingly; in Dylan's very assured hands, the song springs entirely to life.

Even at this late date, people I know – some of them Dylan fans of a certain narrow view, some of them denigrators and trolls – continue to ask, "What the hell does he see in these songs, anyway?" It should be obvious by now that Dylan is drawn to the mechanics of his craft, and found them fascinating enough to surge through the classic songbook a third time.

Certainly, Horace Engdahl of the Swedish Academy understood that songbook's place in Dylan's creative continuum when, in presenting the absent artist with the Nobel Prize for literature in Stockholm on Dec. 10, 2016, he noted, "He is a singer worthy of a place beside the Greeks' ἀοιδόι, beside Ovid, beside the Romantic visionaries, beside the kings and queens of the Blues, beside the forgotten masters of brilliant standards."

Once again Dylan's readings of those standards – knowing, subtle, soulful, amused – came to me at the right time, and they helped me weather the emotional blast of winter, the curious and unanticipated drift of love and time. In this spring I am grateful anew for his companionship.

Released March 31, 2017

Disc I: 'Til the Sun Goes Down
"I Guess I'll Have to Change My Plans"
"September of My Years"
"I Could Have Told You"
"Once Upon a Time"
"Stormy Weather"
"This Nearly Was Mine"
"That Old Feeling"
"It Gets Lonely Early"
"My One and Only Love"
"Trade Winds"

Disc II: Devil Dolls

"Braggin'"
"As Time Goes By"
"Imagination"
"How Deep is the Ocean"
"P.S. I Love You"
"The Best is Yet to Come"
"But Beautiful"
"Here's That Rainy Day"
"Where is the One"
"There's a Flaw in My Flue"

Disc III: Comin' Home Late

"Day In, Day Out"
"I Couldn't Sleep a Wink Last Night"
"Sentimental Journey"
"Somewhere Along the Way"
"When the World Was Young"
"These Foolish Things"
"You Go to My Head"
"Stardust"
"It's Funny to Everyone But Me"
"Why Was I Born"